MW01630007

Duilio Barnabè
1914-1961

I consider Barnabè as the great precursor of
future times, as the artist who will astonish and
mark his epoch with the clearest, noblest and
most accessible language in the world: clearest,
noblest and most accessible language because
of being the most pure.

Jean Bouret
Prisme des Arts, no.19
Paris, 1959

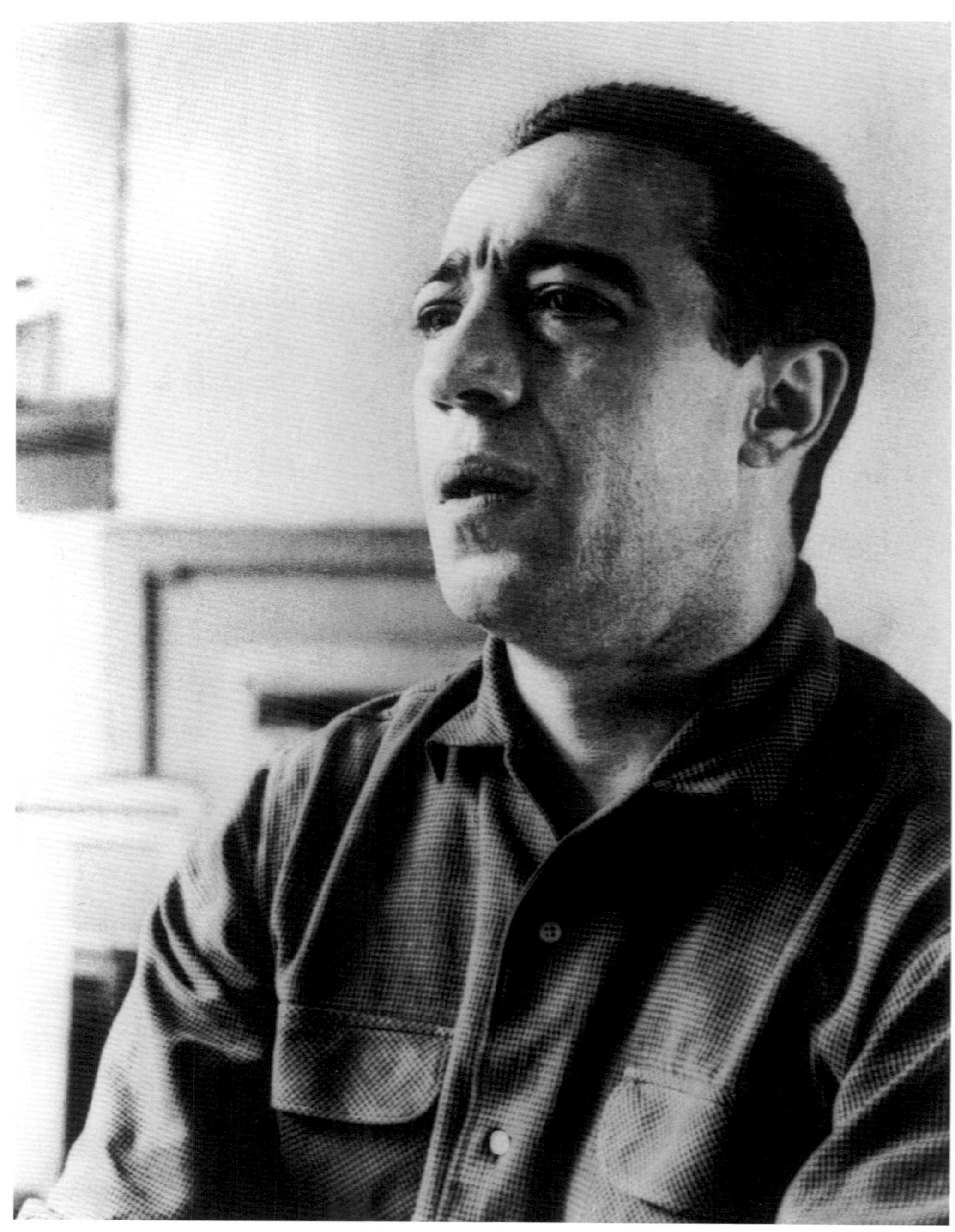

Duilio Barnabè

R. Stanley Johnson

DUILIO BARNABÈ

1914-1961

KLEES/GUSTORF PUBLISHERS
CHICAGO-DÜSSELDORF

Ringraziamo per avere prestato la loro preziosa assistenza:

Paolo Barnabè
Dott. Daniele Barnabè
Dott. Stefano Barnabè
Dr. Geraldine A. Johnson

*

Special Assistance:
Suzanne Smycz
Jacob Fish
Ursula M. Johnson
Gregoire I. Johnson

*

Library of Congress Cataloging Card No. 2003090478
ISBN No. 0-9728927-0-2
Published in Spring, 2003

By the same author
Cubism & La Section d'Or
*Reflections on the Development of the
Cubist Epoch : 1907-1922*
ISBN No. 0-9628903-0-8, 1991

On Cover:
47. *Donna in verde seduta,* about 1956-57
Woman in Green, Seated
Oil on canvas
116 x 89 cm.; 45 3/4 x 35 1/8 inches
Signed lower right

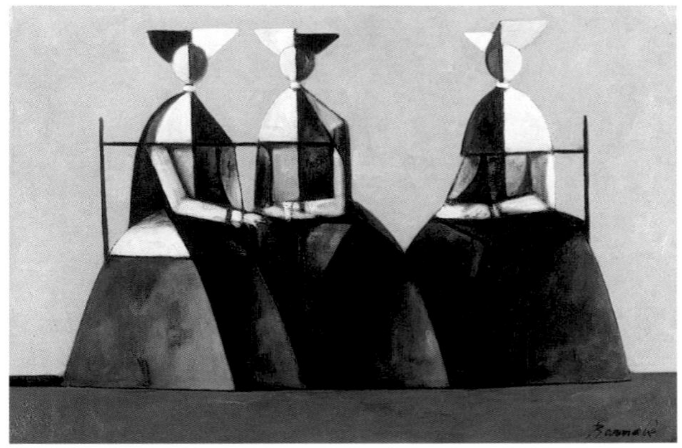

39. *Tre suore* (Three Nuns), about 1956

DUILIO BARNABÈ
(1914-1961)

I. Bologna, Cultural Background : 1914-1946

Duilio Barnabè was born in Bologna in 1914 and at a young age began drawing and painting. His mature artistic achievements date from about 1946 until his early and dramatic death in the French Alps in 1961. This fifteen-year period of creativity began just after the end of *Futurismo*, a movement initiated in Italy by the writer Marinetti in1909 and developed through the early 1940s by artists such as Balla, Boccioni, Carrà and Severini. On the other hand, Barnabè's productive years immediately preceded another influential Italian art movement, *Arte Povera,* which included artists such as Boetti, Kounellis, Merz and Pistoletto and lasted from about 1962 through the mid-1970s. Over the years, Barnabè has been accorded considerable recognition with exhibitions of his works in Bologna, Milan, Triest, Rome, Prague, Copenhagen, Stockholm, Athens, Lisbon, Lausanne, Geneva, London, Paris, New York and Chicago. Barnabè also was selected to present a major exhibition at the 1951 Venice *Biennale.*

*   *   *

Bologna, the city of Barnabè's birth, is the capital of the Emilia-Romagna region and lies in the rich plains at the foot of the Apennines. The center of Bologna still preserves a medieval atmosphere and, in addition to its numerous ancient churches, *piazze* and *palazzi,* the imposing arcades that line the streets give the city a particular elegance. Bologna is known for its university which, already in the twelfth and thirteenth centuries, was one of the most famous and oldest in Europe. In the center of the city is the large, open square formed by the *Piazza Maggiore* and the *Piazza Nettuno.* Around this ensemble are the *Palazzo d'Accursio*, from the thirteenth-century*, and the *basilica di San Petronio. San Petronio,* begun in 1390, dedicated to Bologna's fifth-century patron-saint and decorated with relief sculptures of Jacopo della Quercia, is one of Italy's most impressive religious edifices. As a youth, Barnabè was intimately familiar with this historic center of Bologna, as well as with the neighborhood in the "Saffi" district where his family lived and attended mass at their parish church of *Santa Maria della Grada.*

Even before his art studies at the *Accademia di Belle Arti* in Bologna, Barnabè already had received a stringent religious upbringing. As he matured, however, his intense and questioning nature led him to have doubts about the Catholic religion. At first an ardent believer, he developed an equally strong distrust in his own beliefs. Torn between belief and ironic skepticism, yet remaining sentimentally very attached to the church of his youth, Barnabè's spiritual ambiguities gradually coalesced into a rejection of his early religious upbringing. In many ways, his mental state corresponded to Søren Kierkegaard's religious category of "pure irony".[1] Kierkegaard, whose early nineteenth-century writings were rediscovered by twentieth-century Existentialist thinkers such as Heidegger, Jaspers, Marcel and Sartre, described "pure irony" as a final and necessary religious stage before a God-fearing individual could have the possibility of finding true belief within himself. To become a true believer, from Kierkegaard's point of view, the spell cast in one's youth by Christian dogmatic concepts first had to be completely broken. Only then would it be possible to find an unfettered path to "pure faith".

Whether in the form of "pure irony" or "pure faith", religion, and more precisely the Roman Catholcism with which he was raised, became a great personal problem for Barnabè. Although brought up under the shadow of Bolognese churches in which images of the *Madonna and Child* and *Christ on the Cross* could be found in abundance, significantly he never painted these traditional religious subjects. On the other hand, Barnabè's paintings abound in depictions of figures that were familiar to him as both the physical embodiment and the earthly symbols of religion, namely the cardinals, bishops, nuns, choir boys and others who worked in the service of the Church.

*   *   *

Cultural life in Bologna from the 1920s through the early 1940s was influenced by a regionalist movement called *Strapaese* (super-country).[2] *Strapaese* opposed what were perceived as the "contaminating" effects of modernization and rejected almost all contemporary cultural tendencies (including the then current Cubist approach to the visual arts) that were based on northern European and particularly Parisian ideas about art and literature. With its origins in the idealized, revolutionary days of 1919 before Mussolini came to power in 1922, the proponents of *Strapaese* demanded a return to what were seen as the glories of the Italian past. They defended the "purity" of regional traditions and incited Italians to seek a simpler and healthier provincial life-style. At the time, these objectives were strikingly similar to those of a number of contemporary American artists such as Thomas Hart Benton, John Steuart Curry and Grant Wood. In both of these regionalist movements, the nineteenth century was set in contrast to the twentieth-century, the country to the city, and nature to the machine. *Strapaese*, however, also eventually reflected undertones of the politics of Nationalism and even Fascism. The Bolognese version of *Strapaese* was supported by two local publications: *Il Selvaggio* (The Wild One), edited by Mino Maccari, a close friend of Barnabè's fellow artist, Giorgio Morandi; and *L'Italiano*, published by the writer Leo Longanesi. Ardengo Soffici and Carlo Carrà, who already at the time of World War I had rejected Cubism and urged a return to classicizing values and to "the grand Italian traditions", were the most prominent Bolognese critics defending various aspects of this movement.

Strapaese essentially incorporated two very disparate types of ruralism: one based on solid, traditional Catholic values, the other embodied by "the wild man of the forests" (*il selvaggio*) and characterized by a resistance to all outside influences and controls, from those of the immediate family to those of the Church and the state. Maturing within such criss-crossing and often conflicting beliefs and ideologies, Barnabè's unusually sensitive and receptive personality became marked from early on by a sense of the unresolved and by an inner turmoil that were not particularly apparent, given the artist's relatively tranquil demeanor. These various influences and psychological complexities are reflected in Barnabè's art, for example in the two-sided, divided faces depicted in many of his figural compositions and in the underlying tensions belying the calm surface appearance of many of his still-lifes.

*   *   *

In attempting to relate the art of Barnabè to "the grand Italian traditions", the artist's cultural roots actually could be traced all the way back to the Byzantine mosaics in Ravenna, a city not far from Bologna and even closer to Faenza where the Barnabè family originated before emigrating to Bologna in the mid-eighteen hundreds. In spite of the intervening centuries, the works of the Byzantine masters and those of Barnabè are closely linked by their choice of forms and by related aesthetic sensibilities. In terms of content, however, they are very different. In the art of the Byzantines, stability and universality of form are equated with stability of content. In contrast, within even the most finished works of Barnabè and despite their exterior appearances of total tranquility, subtle elements of instability are always present.

The golden backgrounds of Byzantine mosaics also find parallels in the art of Barnabè, although, unlike the Byzantine masters, his use of a timeless background is consciously chosen. Similar to his Byzantine predecessors, Barnabè's self-imposed, formal restrictions and his purity of line allow his art to reveal underlying, transcendent realities. In seeking such transcendent realities, both the Byzantine masters and many modern artists separate the subjects of their works from the physical reality of the surrounding world, thus leading towards one form or another of abstraction. Barnabè's simplest, most balanced and one could say most "Byzantine" works in fact are his most abstract ones. These works, however, are not "abstract" in the sense of having unrecognizable subjects, but only in their universalized rather than individualized figures and forms. Such abstract and often austere works appear to be the truest expression of Barnabè's artistic strivings and approach closest to his particular sense of reality.[3]

*   *   *

There are a number of formal and thematic links between Barnabè and his well-known contemporary Giorgio Morandi (1890-1964). The two artists were both born in Bologna, though Morandi, who was twenty-four years older, eventually outlived the younger Barnabè. It is notable that the typically delicate colors of Bologna (known as the *Città Rossa* or "Red City") are present in almost every work by Morandi or Barnabè. Both artists found a lifetime of inspiration from the muted roses, faded ochres and dusty yellows that are so prevalent in the coloration of their hometown's streets, buildings and surrounding countryside, as well as in the slate-like blues and grays of the Emilian skies above. Interestingly, the Bolognese scholar and novelist, Umberto Eco, has stated that Bologna's artists can be truly appreciated only after one has "traversed the streets and the arcades of this city and understood that an apparently uniform reddish color can differ from house to house and from street to street." Eco feels there is a "simultaneous quality of homogeneity and diversity" unique to the colors of Bologna.

9

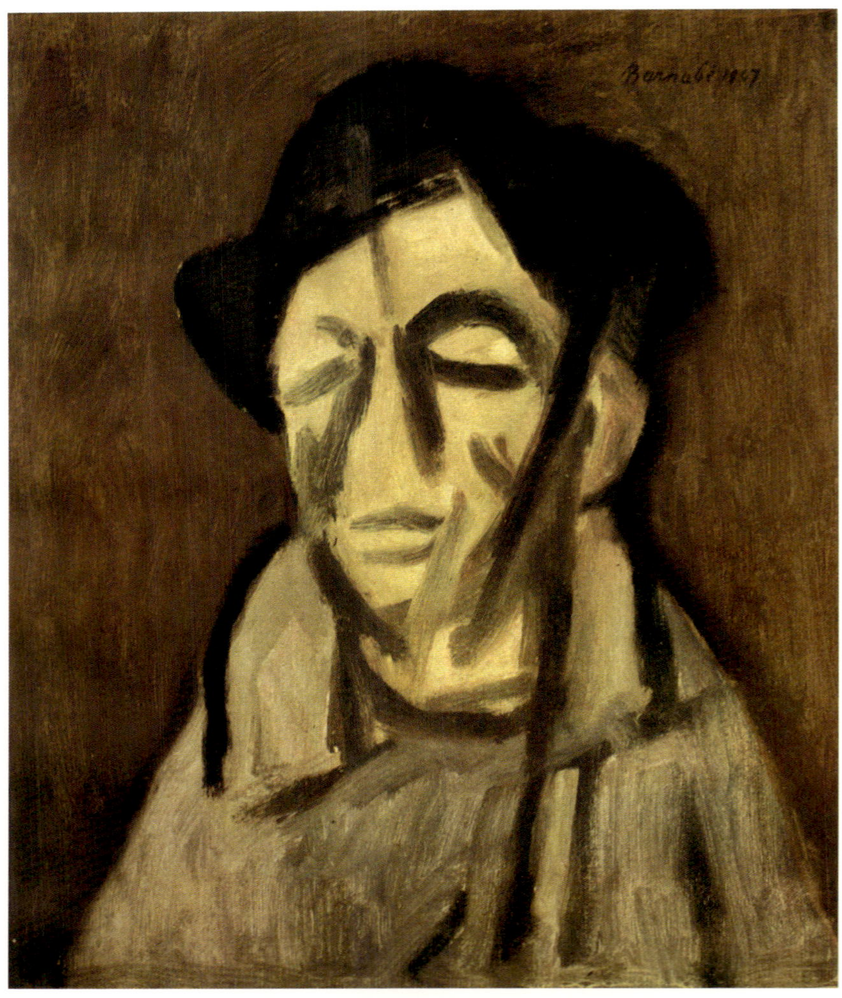

1. *Autoritratto* (Self-portrait), 1947 [4]

Aside from coming from Bologna with its inherent characteristics, the personas of Barnabè and Morandi had little in common. The sheltered, regular life-style of Morandi,who remained a lifetime in Bologna, was very different from that of Barnabè. Barnabè's most productive period consisted of many "unsheltered" years in Paris, where he was subject to artistic influences coming from all over the world. In the case of Morandi, there were no apparent signs of a driven artist, no unsurmontable artistic dead-end streets to overcome, no affairs of intense loves or hatreds, *in summa* none of the mental anguish often associated with the modern artist. As a person and as an artist, Barnabè, on the contrary, was tempetuous, passionate, unpredictable and in a state of constant mental agitation bordering on total dispair.

In their drawings and paintings, Barnabè and Morandi both reveal how under-statement and simplicity can be used as a means to achieve visual complexity. Their understatement and simplicity, however, are derived from different sources. In this respect, though Barnabè spent most of his productive life in France, in many ways he remained more Italian in his art than Morandi. Morandi did not even visit Paris until 1956, but he seems nevertheless to belong more to the French tradition of pure painting, with its love of

10

sensuous brush-strokes and of the vivid materiality of pigments. Contemporary Italian critics did not seem to understand the influence of earlier French masters on Morandi. For example, in 1928, Mino Maccari, the editor of the *Strapaese*-oriented journal *Il Selvaggio,* described the art of Morandi as *italianissima*, with deep roots in Italian tradition. He wrote: "If Italian characteristics are balance and synthesis... purified to simplicity of expression, all are present in Morandi..."[5] This appears, however, to be more a description of the essence of French art, from Poussin and Chardin to Corot and Cézanne, and is very different from the art of either of Barnabè's preferred masters: Mantegna and Picasso. Morandi confirms his views in an autobiographical essay of 1928 in which he stated that: "Among the moderns, in my view, Corot, Courbet, Fattori and Cézanne are the most legitimate of the Italian tradition".[6]

The tightly composed, small-formated subjects of Morandi's art differ greatly from the grand compositional formations found in Barnabè, whose painting is rooted in a truly *italianissima* tradition stretching back to the Renaissance and even to the Byzantine era. It also should be noted that, with only an occasional landscape, Morandi's art was limited almost entirely to still-life painting. Barnabè, aside from a few landscapes, accorded equal attention to figure and still-life. In addition, of these two artists, Barnabè showed the most profound respect for Italy's long artistic tradition of monumentality. Seen already in Byzantine mosaics and then in the massive *Madonnas* of Giotto in the fourteenth-century and again in the imposing figures of Andrea Mantegna and Piero della Francesca in the fifteenth century, this sense of monumentality remains a vital element in many later periods of Italian art. In the twentieth century, this tradition is exemplified by the imaginary, high-walled *palazzi* and isolated gigantic figures dominating grandiose spaces of uninhabited and abandoned *piazze* in the works made from 1914 onwards by the surrealist painter Giorgio De Chirico. The tradition is reaffirmed in the monumentally conceived compositions of Barnabè.

With De Chirico, Barnabè also shared an attachment to an art based on "silence". A great deal of what was important to De Chirico, and then later to Barnabè, is not openly stated in their art, but rather remains intangible, transcendent and often mysterious. Silence, when what is not being said takes precedence over what is said, is a key element in Barnabè's paintings. His figures seem incapable of speaking, his landscapes appear to be far away and soundless, and his still-lifes stand suspended in a dream-like quietness. During Barnabè's most productive period in the 1950s and in the following decade, this sense of painterly silence, not particularly prevalent in contemporary French art, does have interesting parallels in contemporary French literature. This is seen, for instance, in the frequent lack of dialogue in the writings of Jean Genet and Albert Camus as well as in the plays of Paris-based Samuel Beckett. At the end of Beckett's *Waiting for Godot* (first presented in 1953 at the Théatre de Babylone, not too far from Barnabè's Paris studio at the time), the characters Vladimir and Estragon are eternally "waiting for Godot", whoever he was and however he might have been able to help them out of their apparently hopeless situation. As they wait without end, the lives of these two hungry and miserably clothed itinerants appear to be trapped in a "nothingness" with no visible future in sight. In the play, Vladimir's last words are: "Shall we go?" and Estragon replies: "Yes, let's go!". Beckett's final stage instructions are that neither of them should move, that they should continue "waiting", but should remain silent.

*   *   *

In the late 1930s and early 1940s, Fascism reigned in Italy. In terms of controlling cultural activities, however, it took some time for that political movement to exercise total authority. Unlike in Germany, the government initially voiced little objection to styles as diverse as Academicism, Expressionism and Pure Abstraction. There also was a relatively peaceful coexistence between the provincial artistic worlds and the ruling power base in Rome. Mussolini's anti-Semitic and other radical declarations and acts from 1938 on, as well as the pact with Germany in 1939, gradually brought an end to this situation. Whatever hopes for the future, held by more liberal Italians in the early days of Mussolini, were destroyed as the Fascist party grew increasingly powerful, reactionary and nationalistic.

Barnabè was an apolitical individual. However, even in Bologna's relatively calm political situation during the early years of World War II, he was profoundly affected by the increasingly restrictive and threatening atmosphere as well as by the limitations of living in a city which, in spite of its great historical past and cultural institutions, remained provincial and isolated from the world at large. This sense of isolation ended temporarily when Bologna was occupied by the German army in 1943. In 1945, even before the arrival of the liberating allied armies, the city rebelled and expelled the occupying forces at a cost of over two thousand citizens' lives. In 1946, after the dramatic liberation of Bologna, the then thirty-one-year-old Barnabè, together with his young wife, the talented sculptor Angiola Cassanello, decided to leave for Paris. It was there that he spent the remaining and most productive years of his artistic life.

II. Paris, Years of Creation : 1946-1961

Compared to the provinciality of Bologna, the atmosphere of post-war Paris, and in particular the Latin Quarter where the Barnabès lived, was very exciting. For the Barnabès and many other artists and writers, this period proved to be an intellectual and emotional turning point when the ravages of the war years somehow had to be relegated to the past and each individual had to face up to the day-to-day exigencies and often total confusion of life in precarious times with an unpredictable future. For these reasons, public lectures and debates involving the most prominent philosophers in Paris were well attended and the arguments proposed were widely discussed. As Jean-Paul Sartre stated at the time:

> Until recently philosophers were attacked by other philosophers. The public understood nothing of it and cared less. Now, however, they have made philosophy come right down into the market place.[7]

For the Barnabès, in addition to the intellectual stimulations of post-war Paris, there also were the pleasures of living in the Latin Quarter with the Sorbonne, St. Germain-des-Près, boulevard St. Michel, Montparnasse, the endless bookshops, art galleries, *antiquaires, cafés* and remarkable performing personalities such as the novelist and jazz musician Boris Vian and the young, melancholy singer Juliette Gréco. There also was the bristling colony of writers and artists from all over the world. In addition, contemporary art was very accessible for a wide public through three annual art *salons*: the *Salon des Réalités Nouvelles* (the Salon of New Realities), the *Salon de Mai* (the May Salon) and the *Salon des Peintres Témoins de leur Temps* (the Salon of Painters as Witnesses of their Times).

In spite of the seemingly endless distractions and diversions of Paris's intellectual and artistic worlds, for Barnabè the tolling church bells of *San Petronio* in distant Bologna never seemed that far away. In his nature and in the nature of his art, Barnabè remained bound to his Italian roots. In this respect, he was similar to other Italian ex-patriot artists such as De Chirico, Savinio and Sironi whose art, in spite of their long Parisian *séjours*, remained for the most part within the confines of Italy's classical traditions. Barnabè nevertheless was well aware of other artists then living and working in France. His earliest paintings in Paris clearly were influenced by Picasso's Cubist works of 1909-10. Like Picasso, Barnabè, in his painterliness and compositional angularity, in turn also was inspired by Cézanne's still earlier analysis of form. These "cubist" affinities are evident in Barnabè's less conceptual works of 1946-1951, such as his *Ritratto* (Portrait) and *La portinaia* (The Concierge), both of 1948, and his *Figura* of 1950 (plate nos. 2, 4 and 8).[8]

In the later 1940s and the 1950s, the artistic *ambience* of post-war Paris was one of a continuity which saw the resurgence of pre-war masters including Braque, Léger, Matisse and Picasso. The *intelligentsia* of Paris did not show much concern for the *défense* of new, contemporary artistic and literary movements. Under the crushing necessities of daily life, the younger artists and writers at the time were completely preoccupied with themselves as isolated and often hungry creators. Their sentiments and immediate, pressing problems were expressed and examined by a number of French philosophers including Gabriel Marcel (*Être et avoir* was published in 1935), Jean-Paul Sartre (*La Nausée* was published in 1938 and *L'Être et le Néant* in 1943) and Maurice Merleau-Ponty (*Phénoménologie de la perception* was published in 1945). After the horrors of the war and during the uncertainties of the immediate post-war period, these and other European intellectuals felt alienated and alone in what they saw, already in the last years before the war, as an increasingly unstable and threatening world. Echoing the writings of Sartre and Merleau-Ponty, in 1945 the artist Bram van Velde wrote: "Only men who are sick can be artists. It's their suffering which pushes them to do things which put sense back in the world. The sensitive man or the artist can only be sick in our civilized life full of lies....Painting is man's confronting catastrophe...I paint my misery."[9] Seven years earlier, Sartre's novel *La Nausée* (Nausea) presented the imagined diary of a writer who is disturbed by the sickening, chaotic quality of the external world and seeks a universe that is certain and predictable. In creating imaginary worlds which have the formal perfection that the real world lacks, Sartre's writer searches from within his own creativity for solutions to life's problems. Perhaps more than ever before, writers and thinkers based in post-war Paris faced intense, existential dilemmas which forced them to question the very reasons and purposes of their individual creative existences. Barnabè and other visual artists working in this atmosphere similarly strove to find personal meanings, even salvation through their own art.

*   *   *

Barnabè's existential concerns, as expressed through his paintings, are echoed in the works of other post-war artists such as Jean Dubuffet and Nicolas de Staël. Similar to these two artists, Barnabè early on attempted to disentangle himself artistically from his Impressionist, Cubist, Futurist, Expressionist and Surrealist predecessors, thereby trying to break away from the generally backward-looking, art-world

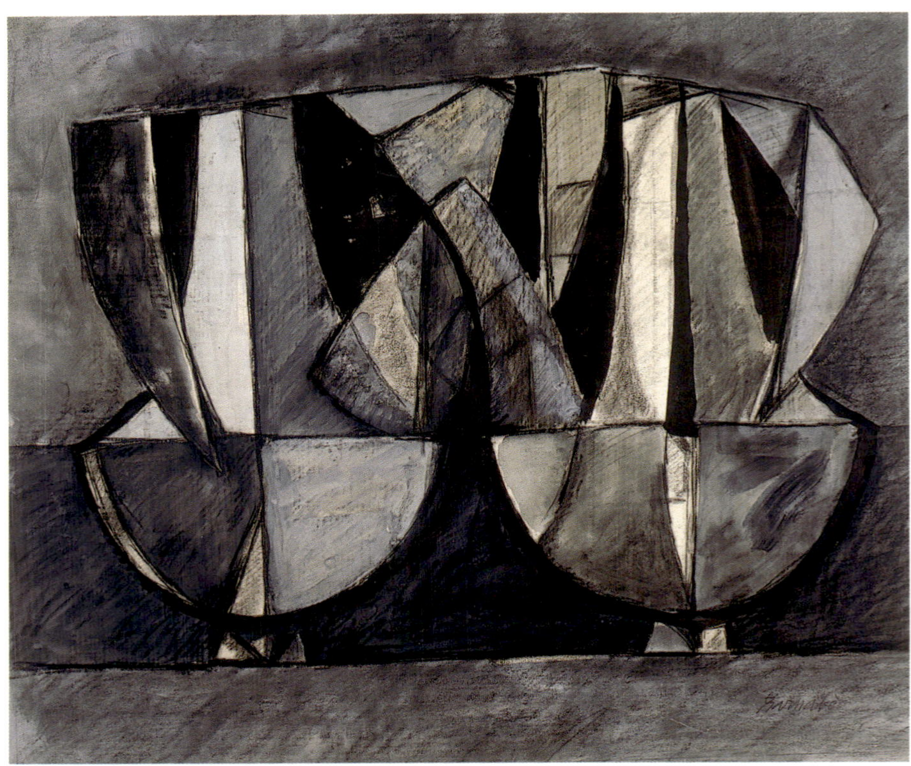

30. *Le due caraffe* (Two Decanters), charcoal and gouache, about 1954

"establishment" of this period. In their art, Barnabè and Dubuffet in particular shared an obsession with relating the trivial to the general, each expressing this obsession in a distinctly different way. Dubuffet, referring to his *Corps de Dame* series, described his painting at the time as one which "brutally juxtaposed the extremely general and the extremely particular, the metaphysical and the grotesquely trivial ...the one... considerably reinforced by the presence of the other." [10] Barnabè, in contrast, concentrated on suppressing the trivial and the particular. For him, what made a person human was not that which made him seem different, but rather that which he had in common with all other human beings. For Barnabè, these were the characteristics which elevated and dignified each individual and gave each individual his or her degree of universality.

In his painting, Barnabè sought conceptual and spiritual values. For him, the deployment of "pure forms" seemed to offer the means to express what he felt to be the essential nature of humanity. For example, the fact that a person's eyes are one color rather than another is less essential for Barnabè than the fact that a person's head is round, since all human heads are round. Barnabè thus eliminated all traces of eye-color in his paintings, but insistently painted heads merely as round forms since this roundness is something he saw as essential to all human beings. It also is essential for human beings to be "doing things". Barnabè thus emphasized the depiction of hands in his figure paintings. Barnabè saw the overall aspect of a figure as more important than single details. He perceived his figures as large, generalized masses whose garments form a single entity with their corporal volumes. Very different from the "synthesis" sought by

14

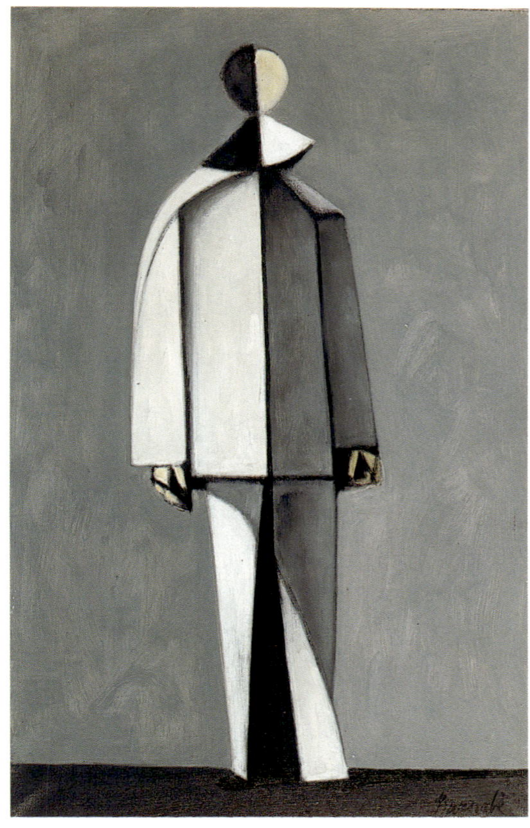

42. *Pierrot,* 1956

de Staël or the "amorphic masses" of Dubuffet, the "masses" of Barnabè, whether in the form of figures, still-lifes or landscapes, are controlled, monumental and usually schematically conceived. They often echo mathematical principles explored from 1912 onwards by the *Section d'Or* (Golden Section) Cubists, including Gleizes, Gris, Metzinger and Villon,[11] and used in different ways by a number of earlier Italian artists, including Severini and Morandi. [12]

Whatever the underlying subjects of his paintings, Barnabè consistently employed similar artistic methods. First, he eliminated what he felt to be nonessential, superficial details and then crystallized what he considered to be the irreducible elements of any given subject. In his search for purity of expression, Barnabè attempted to drive all individual characteristics out of his paintings in order to create abstract, universal emblems. Barnabè's figures, like those of his Parisian contemporary, Alberto Giacometti, are isolated, situated outside of time and devoid of fellow human presence. As in Sartre's "nothingness" or Dubuffet's *Non-lieux* (No-Place) paintings,the monochromatic, cool backgrounds of Barnabè's compositions likewise give no clue about time and place and allow no distinction between past and present.

Barnabè's abstract emblems provided an alternative to the polarized positions associated with mid-twentieth-century debates on realism versus abstraction. His paintings demonstrated that those apparently diametrically opposed positions were no longer adequate by themselves to handle many modern concerns and issues. Instead, Barnabè's art called for a revision of the "heroic" view of modernism as devoid of ideological content and moving inevitably and unstoppably toward total abstraction. In its time, the art of Barnabè, and in various ways also that of de Staël, Dubuffet, Fautrier, Giacometti and a number of other post-war European artists based in Paris, called for nothing less than a general re-orientation of some of modernism's most basic artistic concerns and values.

*   *   *

During the 1950s, when many artists were seeking, in one way or another, to destroy form itself, Barnabè's paintings (except for one short period around 1953 when they veered towards the then common variety of abstraction) evolved instead towards a simplification of forms. There are limits, however, as to how far forms can be simplified. Barnabè's search for abstract symbolism reached a high-point around 1955-57. The next logical development could have been in the direction of Minimalism. Like the painting of Frenhofer in Balzac's novel *Le Chef-d'oeuvre inconnu* (The Unknown Masterpiece), Barnabè's art could have evolved into a series of scribbled lines without any apparent subject or meaning. By about 1958, however, Barnabè was producing paintings that were becoming more descriptive and increasingly "agreeable" in comparison with both the works of many contemporary abstract artists and his own earlier works. Seeing where his painting was headed, Barnabè was most dissatisfied. He sought to extricate himself from what he saw as an ever-narrowing, artistic dead-end street whose facile character did not correspond to the tough and determined nature of his own persona. Barnabè's situation was strangely parallel to that of his Parisian contemporary, Nicolas de Staël. Towards the ends of their lives, both of these artists made increasingly desperate attempts to reverse artistic directions and to return, in one form or another, to more traditional principles similar to those they had rejected earlier. In both cases, their artistic struggles became so all-consuming, emotionally ovewhelming and seemingly hopeless to resolve that each of them finally found suicide to be the only apparent solution to his agonized life.

Barnabè, searching frantically to solve his artistic dilemmas towards the end of his life, tried to return to the ideals of his works prior to 1955-1957. He soon understood that for him such a return to an artistic past was untenable. The increasingly complex and apparently irresolvable problems concerning his art, together with the unrelenting intensity of his moral and religious doubts and struggles, physically and mentally consumed Barnabè in his last years. In the summer of 1960, he visited his mother in Bologna. On October 7th, the night of his forty-sixth birthday, high up in the French Alps on the way back to Paris, Barnabè drove his automobile off the side of a mountain. He miraculously escaped from this accident unharmed. For those of us who knew Barnabè and understood his inclinations and the depths of his despair and who also realized to what extent art was for him more important than life itself, there was a question as to whether this accident really was "accidental". That question was answered one year later when, to the day, again returning from visiting his mother in Bologna, Barnabè drove to a lonely death at exactly the same time of night and at the same turn in the road. This sudden and dramatic end had the same enigmatic quality, the same aura of mystery which characterized Barnabè's entire life and art.

*   *   *

Until recently, Barnabè has been seen as an isolated artist, a special case who did not fit in with any specific movement or group of artists. Other European artists of the period, including Artaud, de Staël, Dubuffet, Fautrier, Giacometti and Richier, have also been viewed as similarly isolated figures. The separation of these artists from one another and from the surrounding artistic world was such that, in the 1940s and 1950s, they were rarely thought of as related by contemporary critics nor brought together in group exhibitions.[13] They did not appear to correspond to a "school" in the same sense as had the Impressionists, the Fauves, the Cubists, the Futurists, the Dadaists, the Expressionists or the Surrealists, the members of each of these groups often meeting to share mutual artistic, social and political ideas and objectives. In the cases of Barnabè and a number of other talented, isolated, mid-century artists, their common ground was precisely their *lack* of shared ideals and objectives, as well as their alienation from one another and from society in general. It was Fautrier who spoke of the "total expansion of being in solitude" and who attempted to establish a fundamental relationship between creativity and the degree of an artist's isolation.[14] There are many critical threads, however, which bring these various artists together, threads which are found already in the writings of a number of the Existentialist philosophers. Among these, Sartre and Marcel in particular attempted to formulate, respectively, possible atheist and Catholic-based solutions for many of the ideological and artistic problems of the post-war generation. One of Barnabè's most fundamental dilemmas, clearly reflected in his art, was his inability to decide between these two Existentialist, but spiritually conflicting points of view.

Barnabè's *oeuvre* stands as one of the more cohesive and powerful bodies of work by a modern artist. His sudden, early death in 1961 seemed particularly tragic in that the extraordinary group of paintings and drawings, he created over the preceding fifteen productive years, appeared to hold such potential and also to anticipate so much that would be developed in later art movements. A noble descendant of Italy's great artistic traditions, Duilio Barnabè in retrospect can now finally be appreciated as a remarkable figure in his own time and as a notable precursor of future art.

R. Stanley Johnson

NOTES

1. See: James Collins, *The Mind of Kierkegaard,* (Chicago, 1965), pp.24, 44, 64-65, 106-107.

2. On *Strapaese,* see: Emily Braun, "Speaking Volumes : Giorgio Morandi's Still Lifes and the Cultural Politics of *Strapaese*", *Modernism/Modernity,* vol.2.3 (1995), pp. 89-99.

3. See: Donna De Salvo and Matthew Gale, *Giorgio Morandi,* (Tate Modern, London, 2001), p. 15, quoting Morandi: "There is nothing more surreal, nothing more abstract than reality", This comment provides an interesting parallel to Barnabè's concept of reality.

4. Plate 1 in: Mario De Micheli, *Barnabè* (Bologna, 1951). Present whereabouts unknown.

5. Joan M. Lukash, *Giorgio Morandi,* (Des Moines Art Center, San Francisco Museum of Art and Solomon R. Guggenheim Museum, 1981-82), p. 34, quoting from: Maccari, *Il Resto del Carlino,* (June 28, 1928).

6. Quoted in: *L'Assalto* (Feb. 18, 1928).

7. Quoted in: Francis Morris, *Paris Post War: Art and Existentialism 1945-55*, (Tate Gallery,London, 1993), p.18, from: J-P Sartre, *Existentialism and Humanism,* (Paris, 1946, London, 1989), p. 58.

8. Illustrated in: Mario De Micheli, *Duilio Barnabè,* (Bologna, 1952), plate nos. 4, 8 and 12.

9. See chapter on Bram van Velde in: Francis Morris, *Paris Post War: Art and Existentialism 1945-55,* (Tate Gallery,London,1993), pp.171-79.

10. See: Jean Dubuffet, *Prospectus et tous écrits suivants II,* (Gallimard, Paris 1967), p.74 as well as Edward Lucie-Smith, *Late Modern: The Visual Arts Since 1945,* (Praeger, New York-Washington, 1969), pp. 90-91. See also: Pierre Schneider "L'immacule conceptuel", *L'Express,* (July 5, 1991), pp. 63-64, quoting Dubuffet: "...éliminer toute présence humaine, toute trace de l'intervention d'une main (ou d'une conscience), à boire à la source de l'absence" ("eliminate all human presence, all traces of the intervention of a hand (or of a conscience) and to drink from the source of Absence").

11. See: R. Stanley Johnson *Cubism & La Section d'Or,* (Chicago and Düsseldorf, 1991), pp. 7-28.

12. E.g.: Severini's *Portrait of F. T. Marinetti,* 1912-1913, *Portrait of Paul Fort,* 1913, *Plastic Rhythm of July 14th,* 1913, *La Ciociara,* 1914, and *Plastic Synthesis of the Idea of "War",* 1915(see: Severini : *The Life of a Painter,* Princeton, 1995 : plate nos.22, 21, 33, 32 and 35); and Morandi's *Flowers,* 1916 (Pinacoteca di Brera, Milan) and *Still Life,* 1916 (Museum of Modern Art, New York), (see: *Giorgio Morandi,*Des Moines Art Center, San Francisco Museum and Solomon R. Guggenheim Museum, 1981-82: plate nos.5 and 6, on pp.90-91).

13. An exception to this was the exhibition organized in 1951 by jazz musician, sculptor and art entrepreneur Michel Tapié. With the title of *Les Signifiants de l'Informel* (Significant "Informal" Artists), this at the time largely unnoticed exhibition took place in Paris at the small Latin Quarter Galerie Nina Dausset and brought together six artists: Dubuffet, Fautrier, Georges Mathieu, Michaux, Riopelle and Iaroslav Serpan. Refering to this exhibit, see: Francis Morris *Paris Post War: Art and Existentialism 1945-55*, (Tate Gallery, London, 1993), p. 21.

14. Quoted in: Francis Morris *Paris Post War : Art and Existentialism 1945-55*, (Tate Gallery, London, 1993), p. 20, from: Sarah Wilson "Jean Fautrier : Orthodoxy and the Outsider", *Art International,* vol. 4 (Autumn, 1988), pp.13-40 and 35.

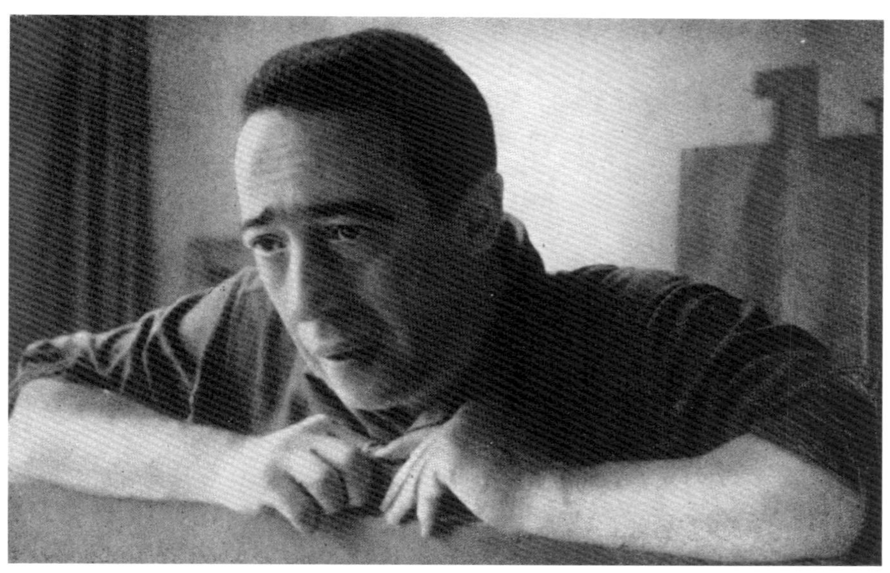

BIOGRAPHIC NOTES, EXHIBITIONS, PUBLICATIONS

1914 - Duilio Barnabè born in Bologna, Italy. The family was originally from the small town of Faenza, near Ravenna on the Adriatic coast in the northern province of Emilia-Romagna. Faenza was famous for its ceramics and in fact is the origin of the French generic term *faience*. Around 1852, the Barnabès moved from Faenza to the "Saffi" district of Bologna. There, Barnabè's grandfather, Giuseppe Barnabè, and then his father, Mario Barnabè, were shop-keepers. Barnabè's mother, Eugenia Santi, was from Bologna. Barnabè's brother Paolo also was a shopkeeper in Bologna. Paolo's two sons (Duilio Barnabè's nephews), Daniele and Stefano, both became doctors in Bologna. The Barnabès were Catholic. Their parochial church was *Santa Maria della Grada* in the "Saffi" district of Bologna. From an early age, Barnabè showed great interest in drawing and painting. He eventually studied art at the Accademia di Belle Arti in Bologna where Giorgio Morandi was one of his teachers.

1935 - To fullfill his military service obligations, Barnabè joined the Italian army and served as a Lieutenant in Tobruck in North Africa.

1938 - At the age of 24, Duilio married another young artist from Bologna, Angiola Cassanello.

1940 - Called back into the army and served in Lubiana (Slovenia). Succeeded in leaving the army and returned to Bologna to devote himself entirely to his art.

1941 - At age 27, received the Barruzzi Prize for Contemporary Art. Executed frescos for the Civic Theater in Adria, a small town near Venice. Worked together with the glassmaker Fontana in Milan. This resulted in numerous works in ceramics and then later (in 1955) in his commission to execute stained-glass windows for the votive church of *S. Nicolao della Flue* in Lugano.

1943 - Received the International Curlandese Prize for Fine Art.

1946 - Barnabè and his wife leave for Paris.

1947 - Exhibit at the Galleria de Cavallino, Venice.
Exhibit at the Galleria Cupola, Bologna.
Participated in exhibit of *Italian Contemporary Art*, Kunsthalle, Bern, Switzerland.

1948 - Exhibit at the Galleria Naviglio, Milan.
Exhibit at the Galleria della Scorpino, Triest.
Participated in the international *Quadriennale* of Rome and the Venice *Biennale*.
Received the yearly Prize for Contemporary Art of the City of Milan.

1949 - Exhibited at the Galleria del Secolo, Rome

1950 - Exhibit at the Galleria Antico Martini, Venice.
Participated in exhibit on *Modern Italian Art*, Prague, Czechoslovakia.

1951- Publication of book: *Duilio Barnabè* by Mario De Micheli, (Edizioini d'Arte Licinio Cappelli, Bologna, 1951).

1952 - A major solo exhibit at the *Biennale,* Venice.

1953 - Under the patronage of the *Biennale* of Venice, exhibited in both Athens and Lisbon.
Exhibited at the Galerie Blanche in Stockholm and Halsinborg, Sweden.

1954 - Exhibit at the Galerie Birch in Copenhagen.

1955- Executed stained-glass windows for the votive church of *S. Nicolao della Flue* in Lugano for which he received a Gold Medal award from the Ministry of Education in October, 1955.

1956 - Exhibit at the Galerie Barbizon, Paris.

1957 - Exhibit at the Musée de l'Athénée, Geneva, Switzerland.
Exhibit at the Galerie Barbizon, Paris.

1958 - Exhibit at the Galerie Bettie Thommen, Basel, Switzerland.

1959 - Publication of *Duilio Barnabè,* with documentation brought together by Ivan Bettex and introduction by Guy Dornand, *Les Cahiers d'Art - Documents*, No. 97 (Editions Pierre Cailler, Geneva, Switzerland, 1959).
Exhibit at the Galerie Visconti, Paris.
Participated in a group exhibition in London.
Exhibit at the Galerie Paul Vallotton, Lausanne, Switzerland.
Exhibit at the Musée de l'Athénée, Geneva, Switzerland.

1960 - In 1960 and 1963, the Chicago gallery of the late S. E. Johnson (1904-1967) presented the first exhibitions of Barnabè in the United States. From these two exhibitions, works entered the collections of Kirk Douglas, Burt Lancaster, Edward G. Robinson, Gene Kelley and the Hollywood director John Negulesco.

1961 - Barnabè spent the summer in Italy. This was a period when Barnabè was physically and mentally consumed by a variety of personal problems as well as unending questions involving the direction of his art. On his return to Paris, while driving through the French Alps near the Swiss border, Barnabè had a fatal automobile accident which ended his life.
Barnabè was buried in the family tomb in the cemetery in Bologna.

1976 - Between 1976 and 1991, three exhibitions were presented by R., S. Johnson Fine Art in Chicago: *Homage to Duilio Barnabè*, 1976; *Barnabè in Retrospect,* 1981; and *Duilio Barnabè: A Homage Presented on the Thirtieth Anniversary of the Death of the Artist* (including works from the Collection of Mr. & Mrs. Kirk Douglas), 1991.

SELECTED BIBLIOGRAPHY

Ivan Bette	*Duilio Barnabè, Les Cahiers d'Art-Documents,* no. 97 (Geneva, 1959).
Jean Bouret	"Barnabè", *Prism des Arts* (Paris, 1959).
Emily Braun	"Speaking Volumes : Giorgio Morandi's Still Lifes and the Cultural Politics of *Strapaese*", *Modernism/Modernity,* vol. 2.3 (1995), pp. 89-116.
Waldemar George	Prefaces, *Barnabè* (Musée de l'Athenée, Geneva, 1957 and 1959).
Robert Hellebranth	Preface, *Barnabè* (Galerie Barbizon, Paris, 1956).
Regnar Hoppe	Introduction, *Barnabè* (Galerie Birch, Copenhagen, 1954).
R. Stanley Johnson	Prefaces: *Barnabè* exhibitions (R. S. Johnson Fine Art,Chicago, 1976, 1982, 1991).
S. E. Johnson	Prefaces: *Barnabè* exhibitions (Johnson International Gallery,1960, 1963).
Joan Lukach, Amy Worthen et al	*Giorgio Morandi* (Des Moines Art Center, San Francisco Museum of Center Modern Art and Solomon R. Guggenheim Museum, 1981-82).
Mario De Michele	*Duilio Barnabè (*Edizioni d'Arte Cappelli, Bologna, 1951).
Francis Morris	*Paris Post War: Art & Existentialism 1945-55* (Tate Gallery, London,1993).
Rodolfo Palluchini	Preface, *Barnabè* (Galerie Blanche, Stockholm, 1953).
Mario Ramous	*Testimonianze per un Cammino* (Galeria del Naviglio, Milan, 1948).
Donna De Salvo & Matthew Gale	*Giorgio Morandi* (Tate Modern, London, 2001).
Gino Severini	*Gino Severini : The Life of a Painter* (translated by Jennifer Franchina, Princeton, 1995; originally published in Italian with the title of *La Vita di un Pittore,* Giangiacomo Feltrinelli Editore, 1983).
Giulio Tavernari	*Capitolo per Barnabè* (Galeria del Cavallino, Venice, 1947).
Tristano Varni	"Artisti d'oggi - Duilio Barnabè", in *Il Pomeriggio* (Bologna, 1951).
Carlo Volpe	*Duilio Barnabè* (with a limited edition of five lithographs, Edizioni d'Arte Cappelli, Bologna, 1952).
Robert Vrinat	"Barnabè", in *Le Jardin des Arts*, no. 23 (Paris, July 1957).

SELECTED CRITICAL COMMENTS

From one abandonment to another, Barnabè has arrived at a culminating point in art. His visages, having lost their history of seeing, eating and breathing humanity, have become essentially only the refuge of the soul. It is still man, who inhabits the object just as easily as a cathedral. With grays coldly posed and without any deformation in the painting form itself, Barnabè in broad, flat forms constructs works which can only be considered as monumental whether their actual size be large or small. For Barnabè would seem to be reserved the most brilliant artistic future.

Jean Chabanon
Le Peintre, Paris

Barnabè is a painter of conciliation and of silence, a painter of the impossible dialogue. He poses the problem of communication in the barest and nudist plastic terms, confounding willingly the animate and the inanimate.

Michel Concil-Lacoste
Le Monde, Paris

Barnabè sets himself apart from the typical forms of contemporary art. Nothing which is human is foreign to him. The lively and active humanism which he expresses does not merely derive from the plastic repertory bequeathed by the past. It is an affirmation of the presence of man and of his supremacy.

Waldemar George
Preface to *Barnabè* exhibit catalogue,
Athena Museum, Geneva, Switzerland

PLATES

1. ***Autoritratto,*** 1947
   Self-portrait

   Oil on canvas
   41 x 34 cm.; 16 1/8 x 13 inches
   Signed and dated, upper right

   Literature:
   Mario De Micheli *Dulio Barnabè*, Edizioni d'Art Licinio Cappelli, Bologna, 1951: no. 1 and
   reproduced in color.

   (reproduced on page 10)

2. ***Nudo,*** 1948
   Nude

   Oil on canvas
   100 x 65 cm.; 39 3/8 x 25 5/8 inches
   Signed and dated, upper right

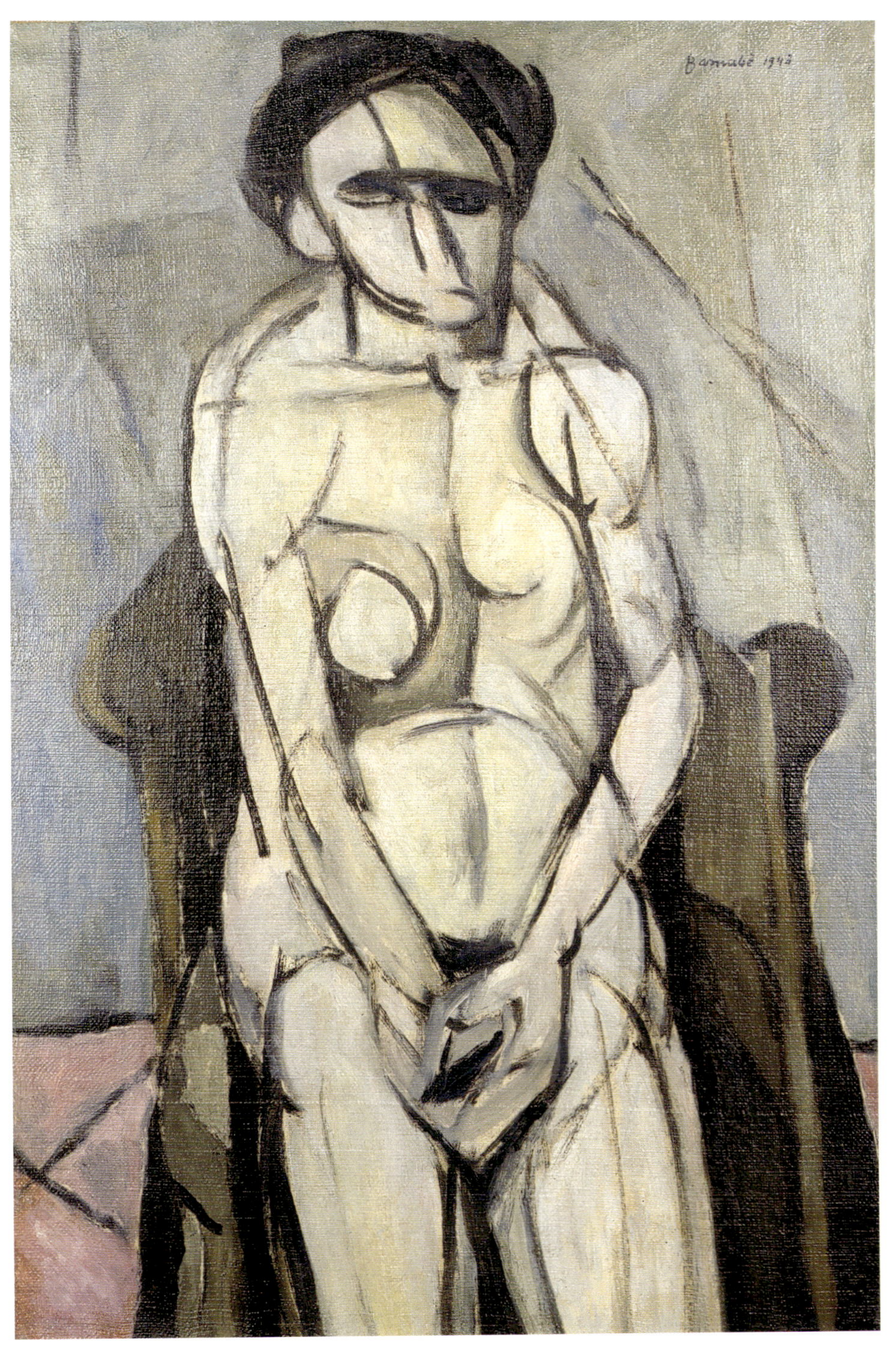

3. ***Ritratto,*** 1948
   Portrait

   Oil on canvas
   65 x 49 cm.; 26 3/4 x 19 1/8 inches
   Signed, upper right

   Literature:
   Mario De Micheli *Dulio Barnabè*, Edizioni d'Art Licinio Cappelli, Bologna, 1951: no. 4 and
   reproduced in color.

   Collection:
   Private collection

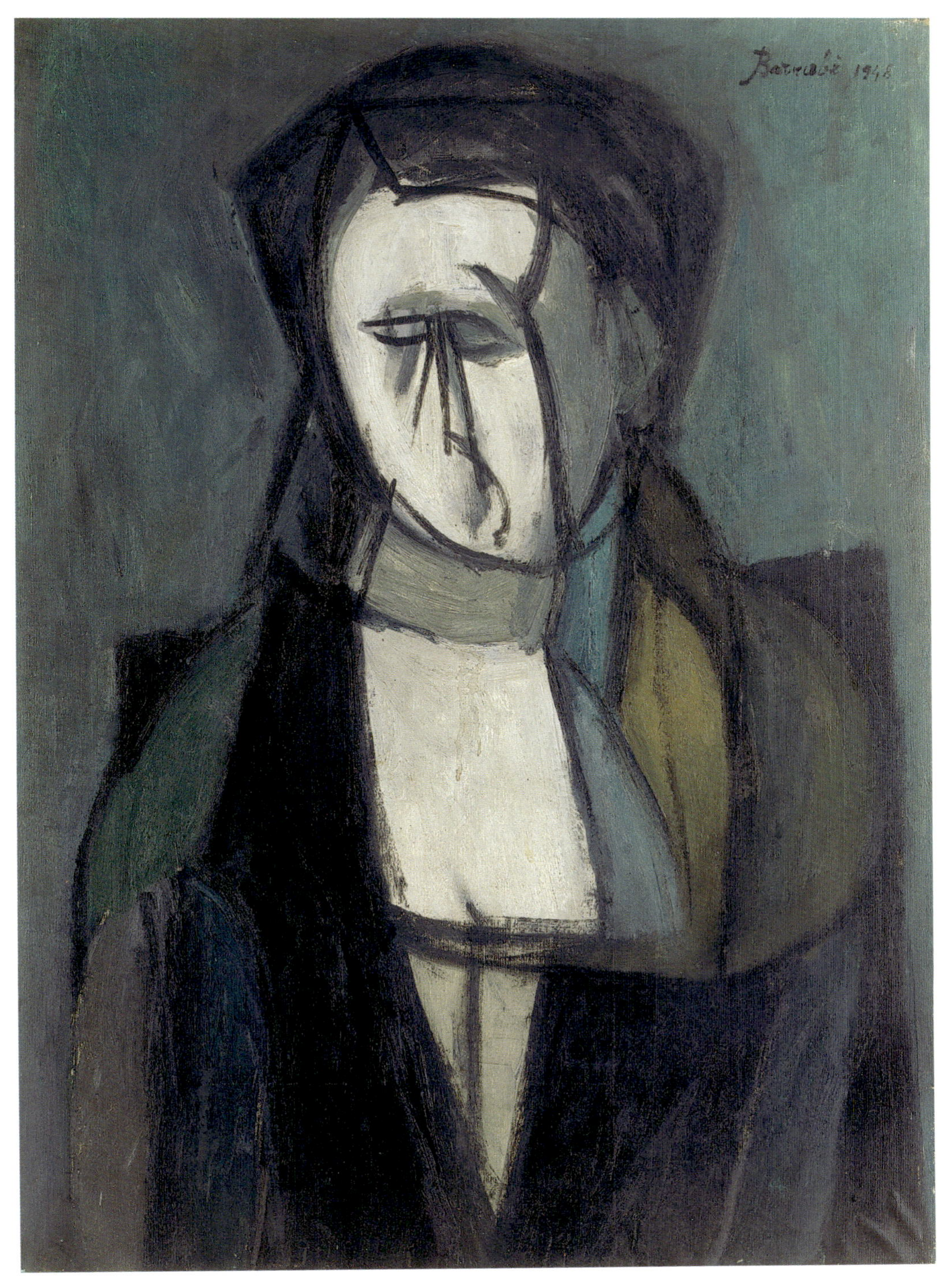

Barnabé 1946

4. ***Uomo con cappello,*** 1948
    Man with Hat

    Oil on board
    70 x 48 cm.; 27 1/2 x 19 inches
    Signed and dated, upper left

    Collection:
    Rick and Susan Sontag

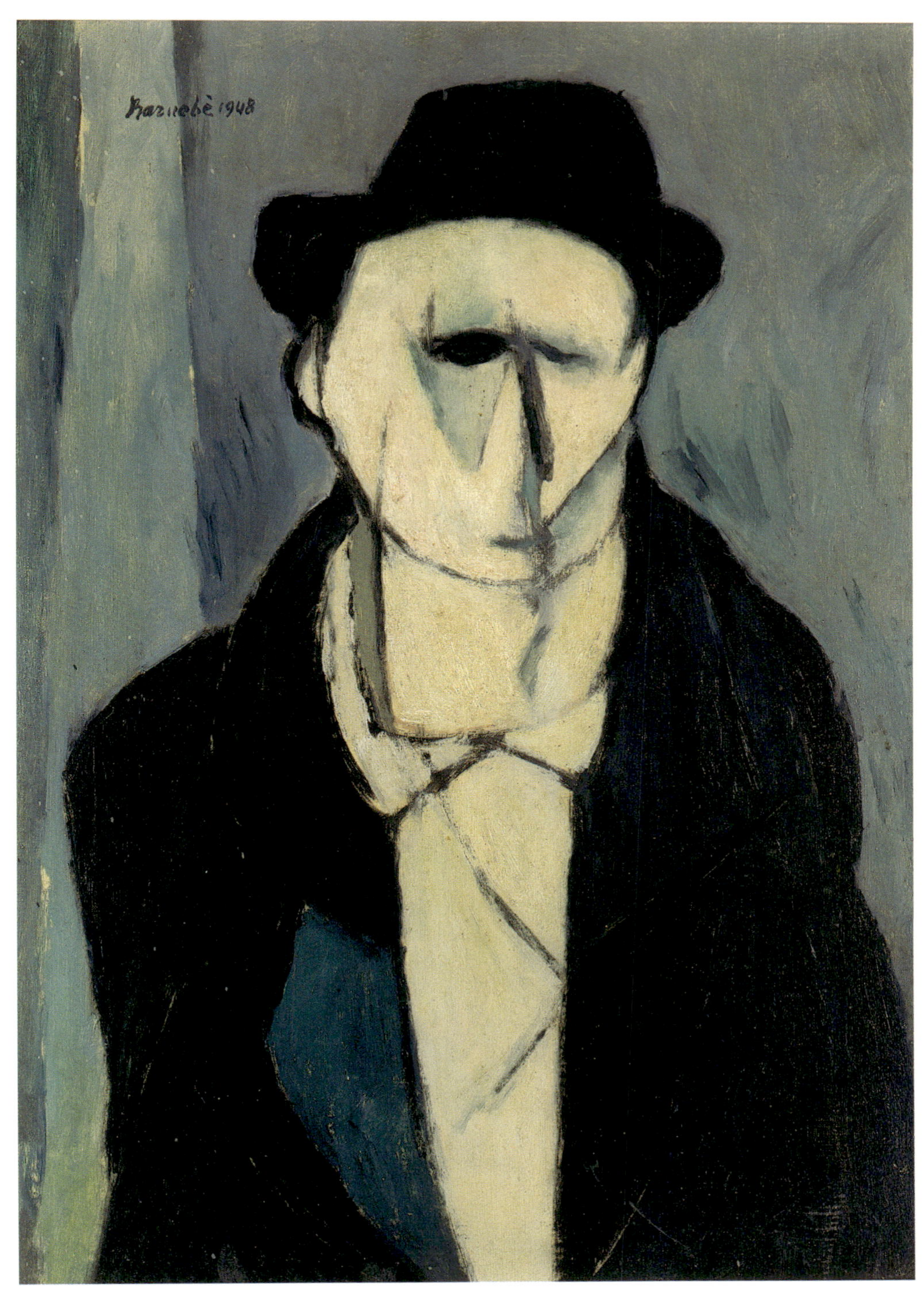
Barnabè 1948

5. ***Figura seduta*** or ***la portinaia,*** 1948
    Sitting Figure or The Concierge

    Oil on canvas
    156 x 97 cm.; 60 3/4 x 38 3/4 inches
    Signed and dated, upper right

    Literature:
    Mario De Micheli *Duilio Barnabè* Edizioni d'Arte Licinio Cappelli, Bologna, 1951: no. 8 and
    reproduced in color.

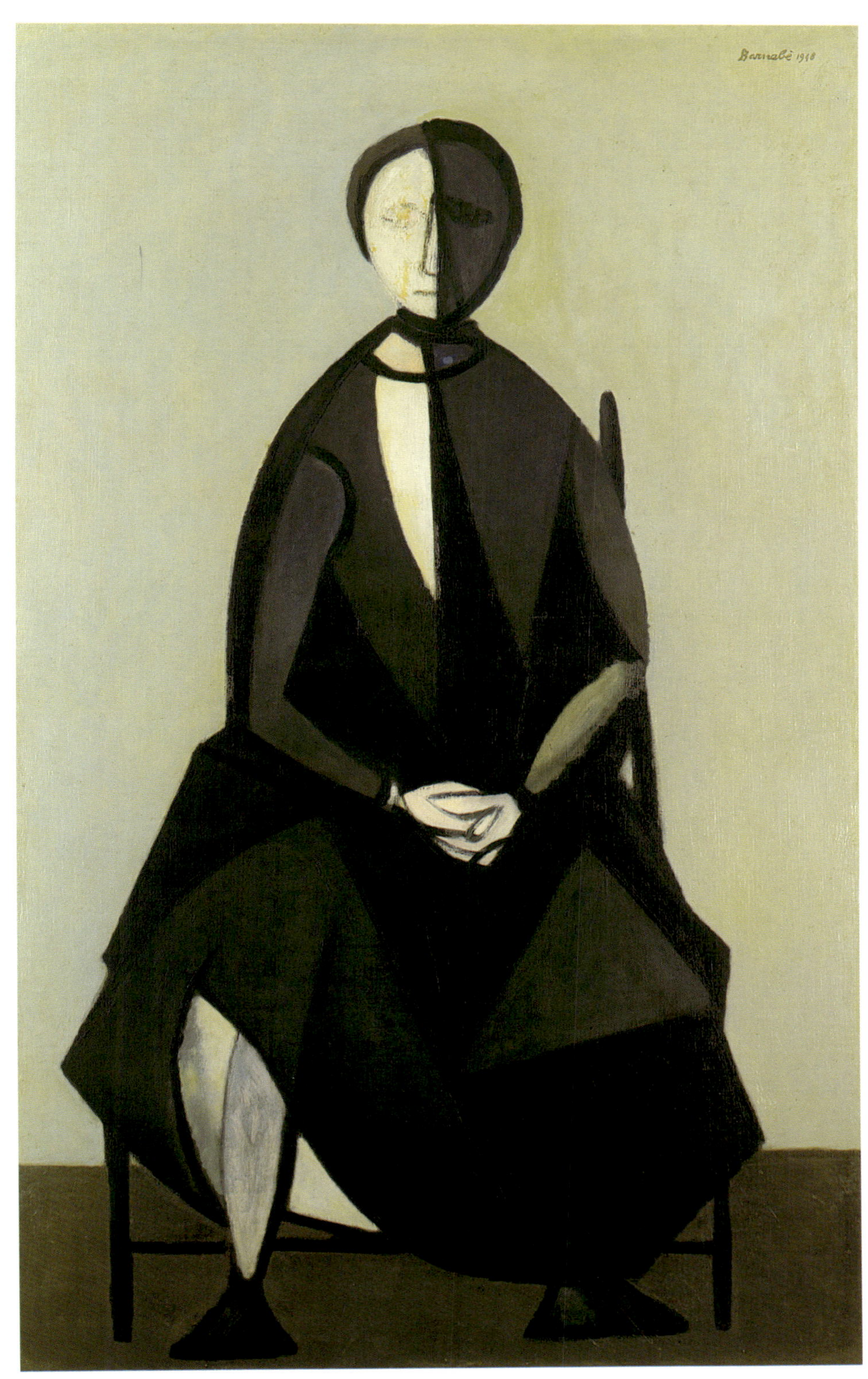

Barnabé 1958

6. ***Figura seduta,*** 1949
   Seated Figure

   Oil on canvas
   60.3 x 50.2 cm.; 23 3/4 x 19 3/4 inches
   Signed , lower right, and signed, titled and dated on reverse

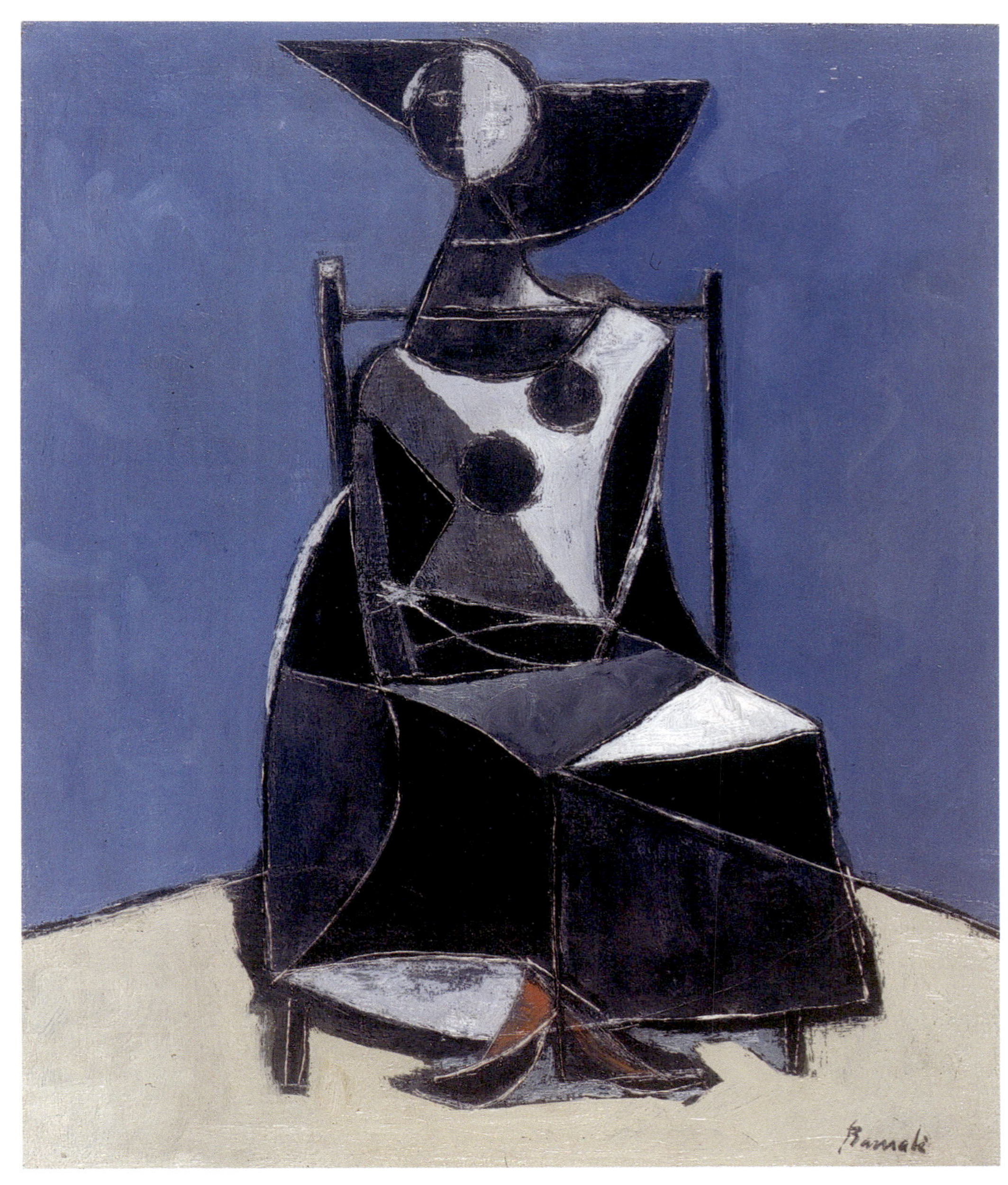

7. ***Figura seduta, fondo nero,*** 1950
    Sitting Figure: Black Background

    Oil on canvas
    105 x 75.5 cm.; 41 1/2 x 29 3/4 inches
    Signed and dated, upper right.

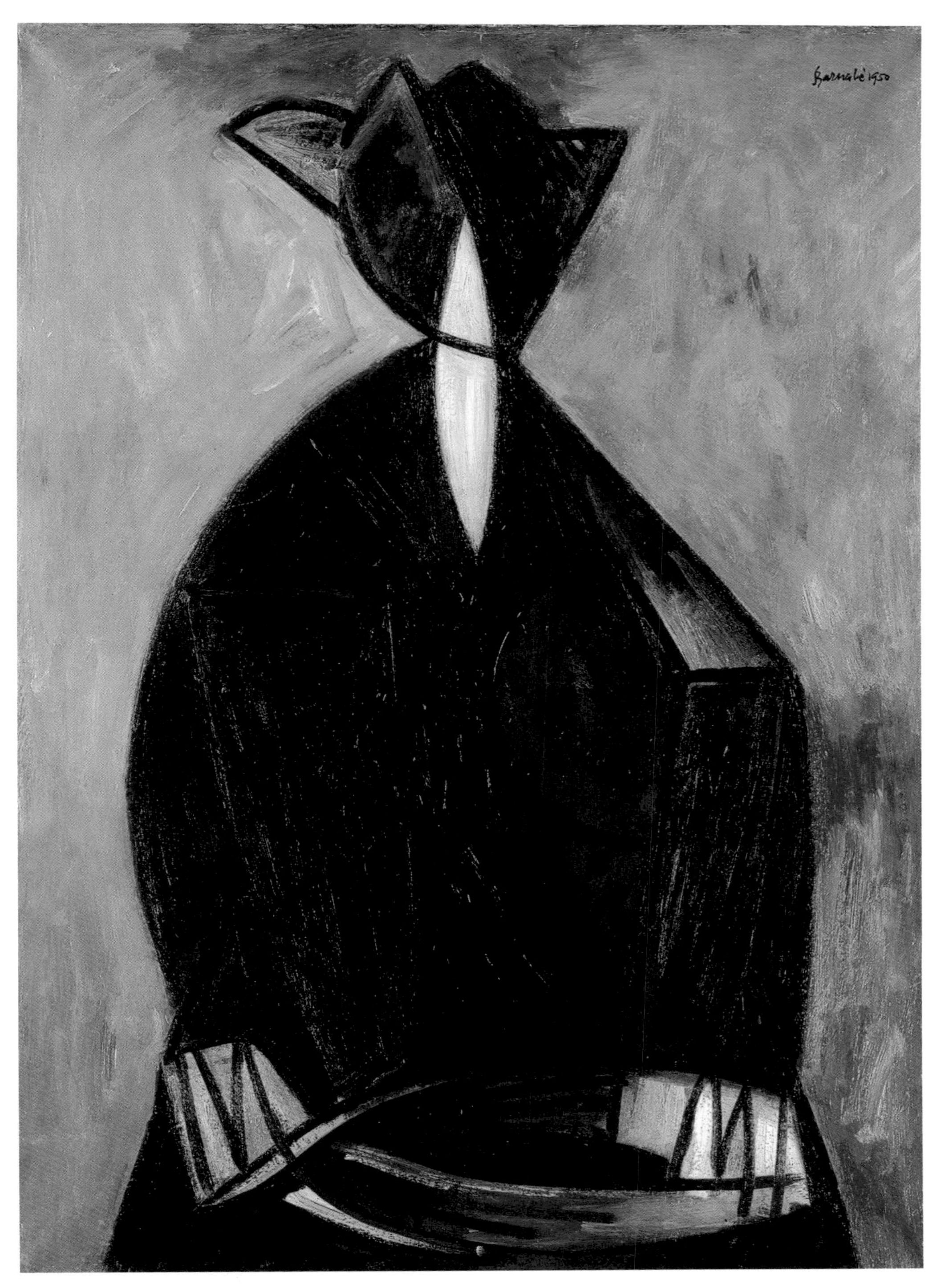

8. ***Natura morta,*** 1950
   Still Life

   Oil on canvas
   54 x 81.3 cm.; 21 1/4 x 32 inches
   Signed and dated, upper right

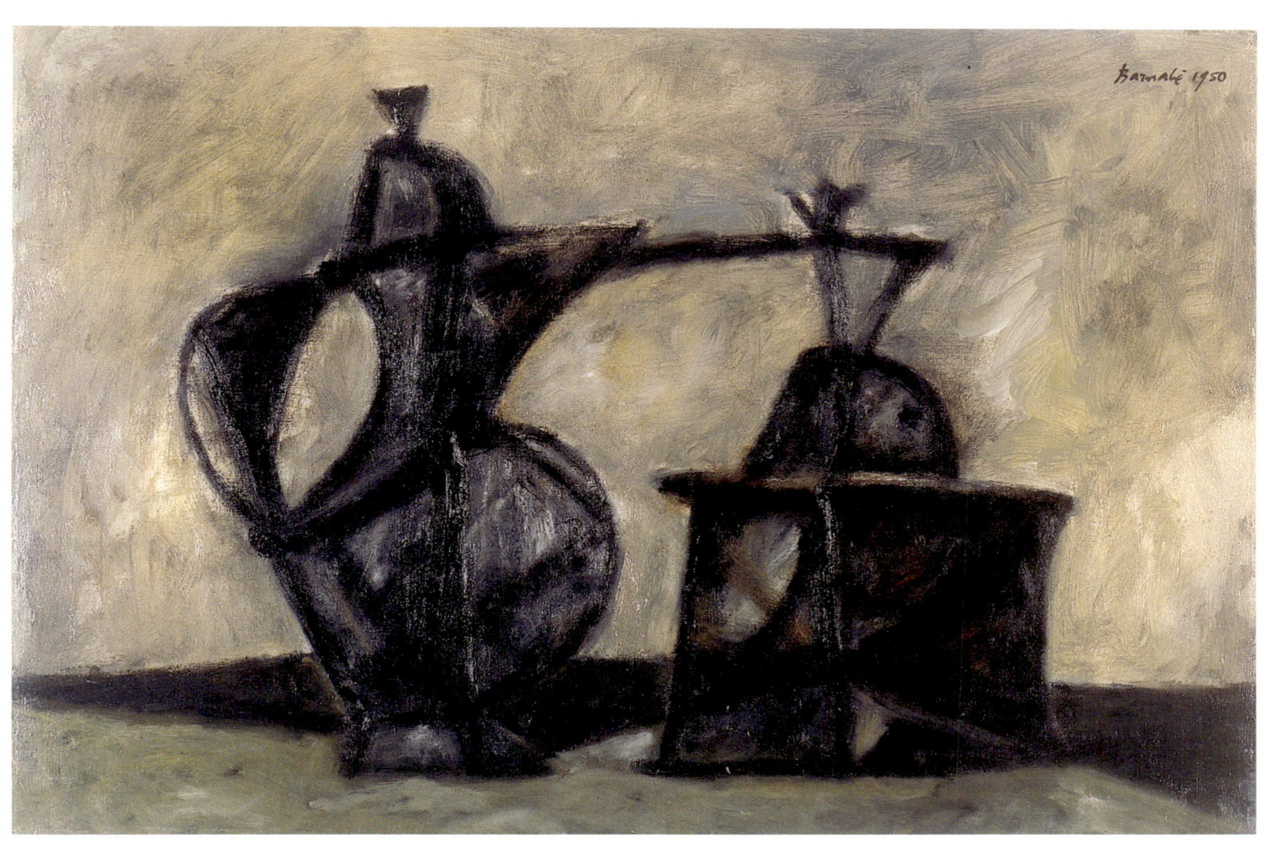

Barnabé 1950

9. ***Figura,*** 1950
Figure

Oil on canvas
98 x 82 cm.; 38 3/4 x 32 3/8 inches
Signed and dated, upper right

Literature:
Mario De Micheli *Duilio Barnabè*, Edizioni d'Art Licinio Cappelli, Bologna, 1951: no. 12 and
reproduced in color.

Collection:
James Anderson and Donald Baron

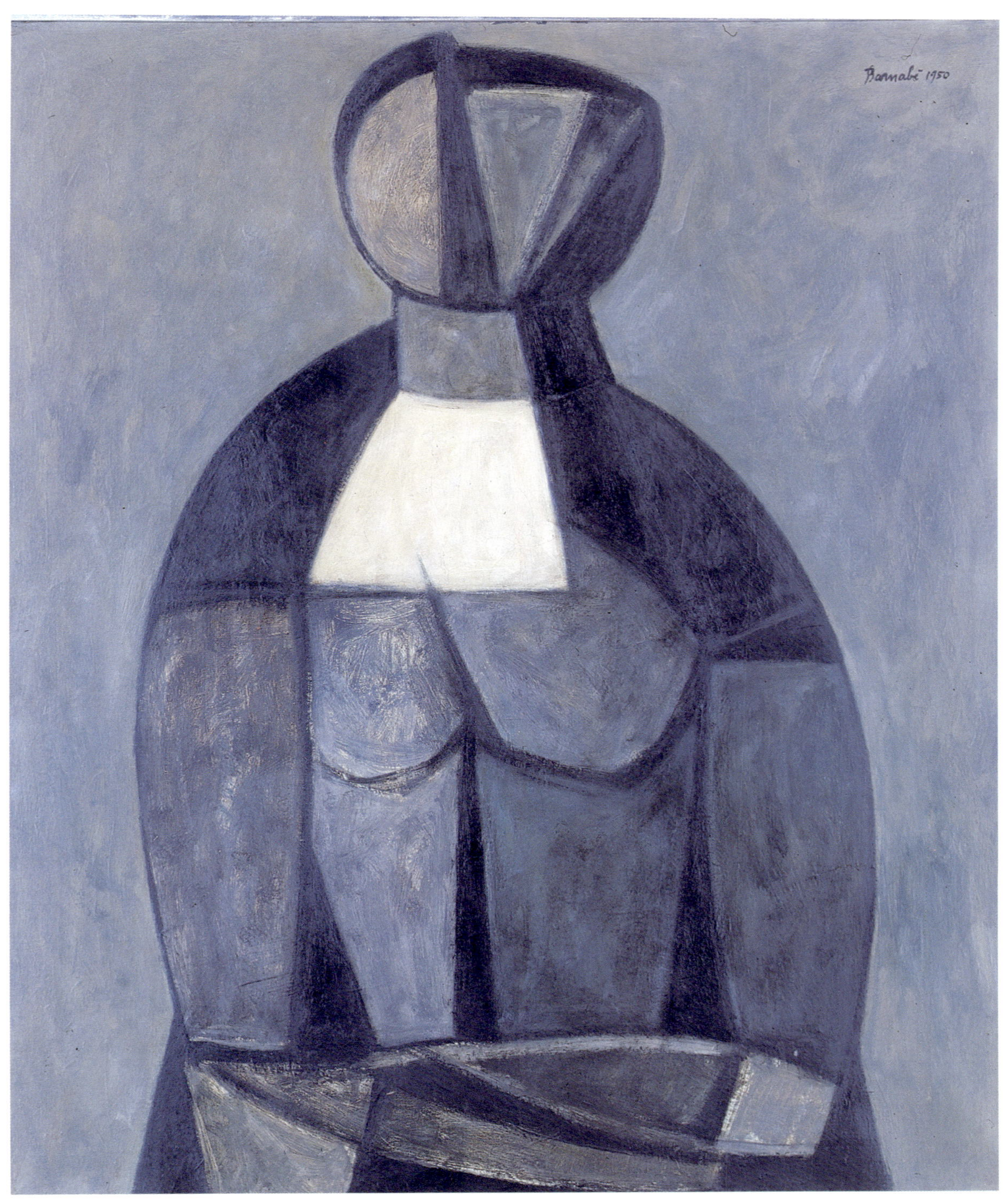

10. ***Figura seduta,*** about 1950
Seated Figure

Oil on canvas
100 x 55 cm.; 39 1/4 x 21 5/8 inches
Signed, upper right

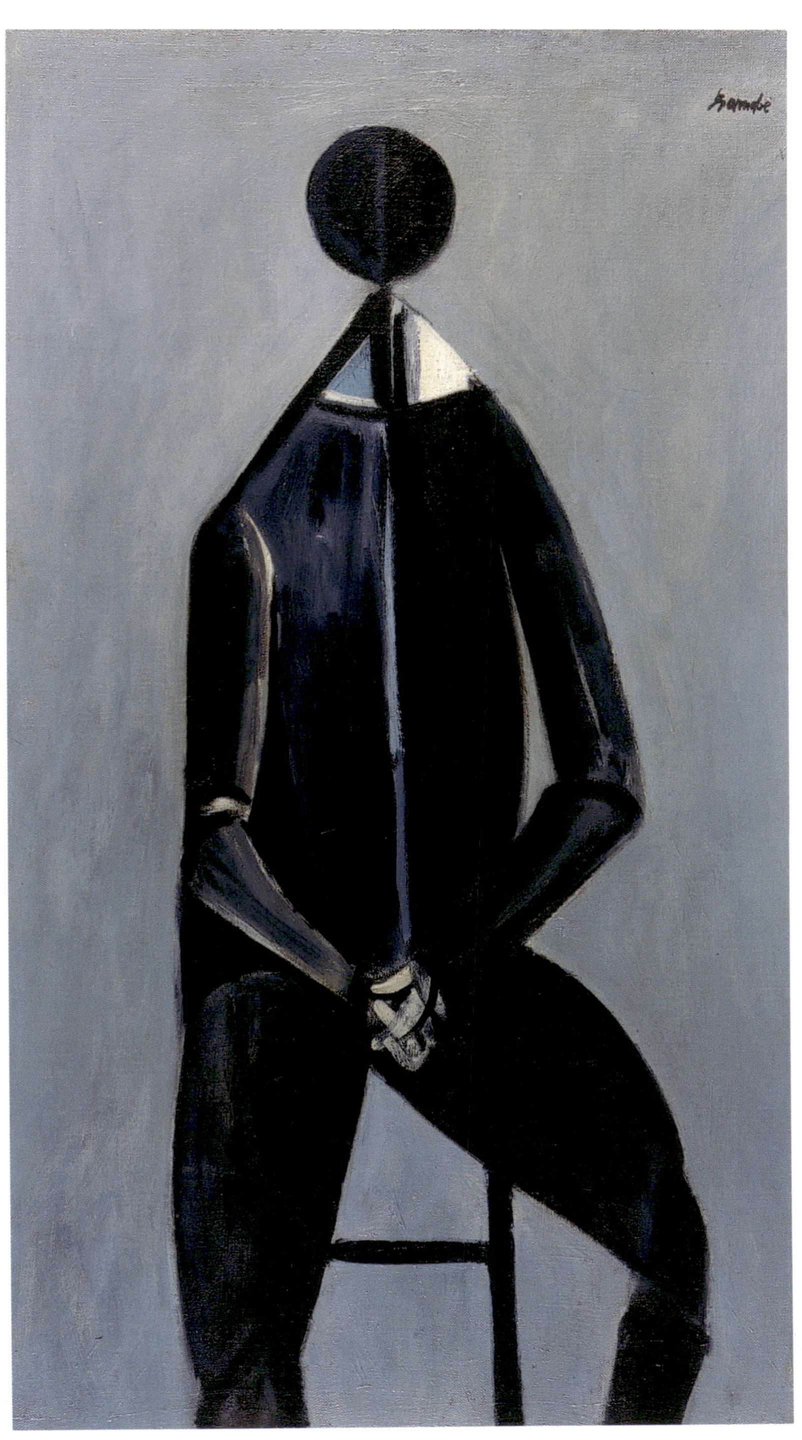

11. ***Figura seduta, fondo blu,*** 1950
    Sitting Figure: Blue Background

    Oil on canvas
    100 x 68 cm.; 39 1/2 x 26 15/16 inches
    Signed and dated, upper right

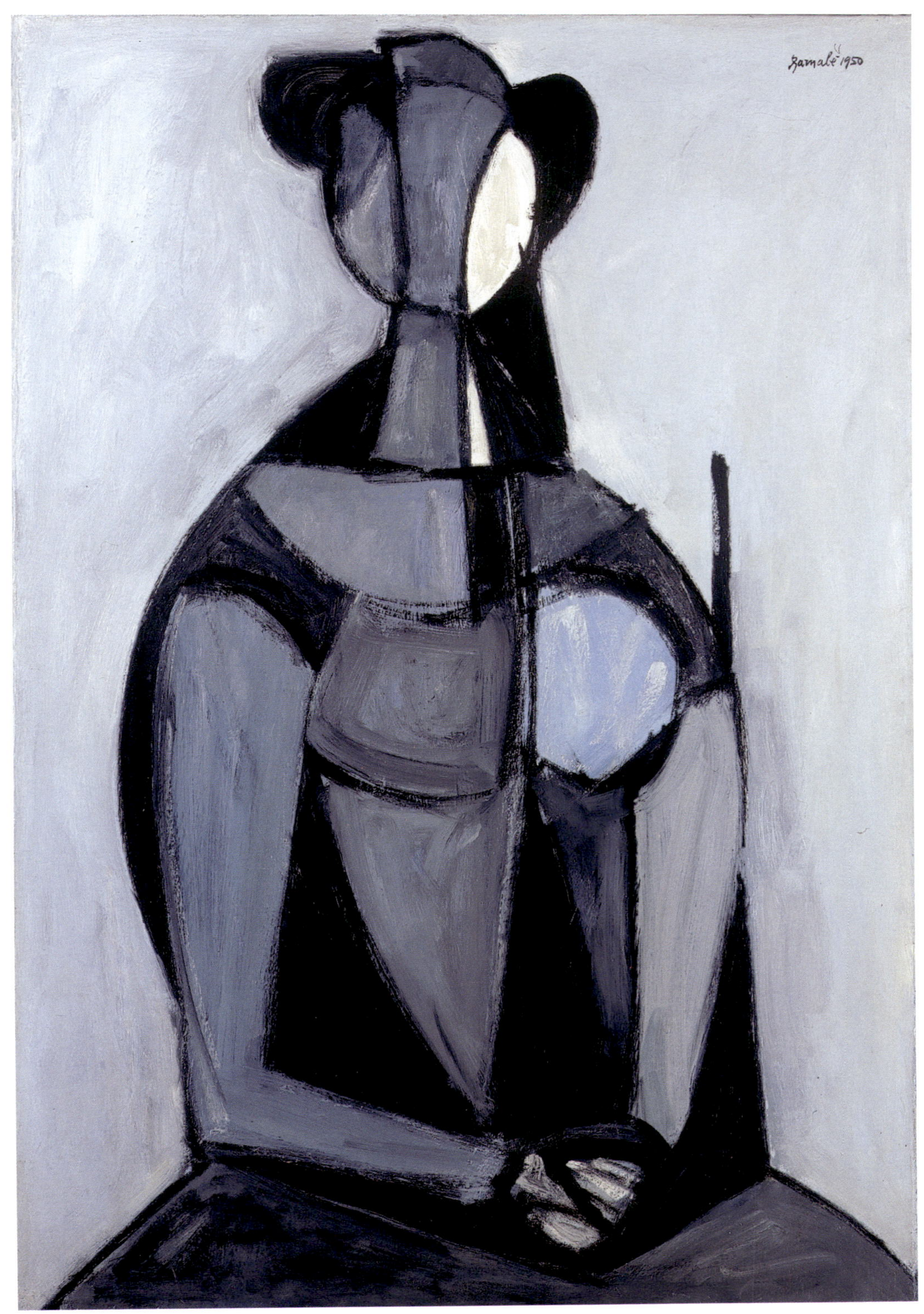
Zamalé 1950

12. ***Natura morta,*** about 1950
    Still Life

    Oil on canvas
    73 x 91.4 cm.; 28 3/4 x 36 inches
    Signed, lower right

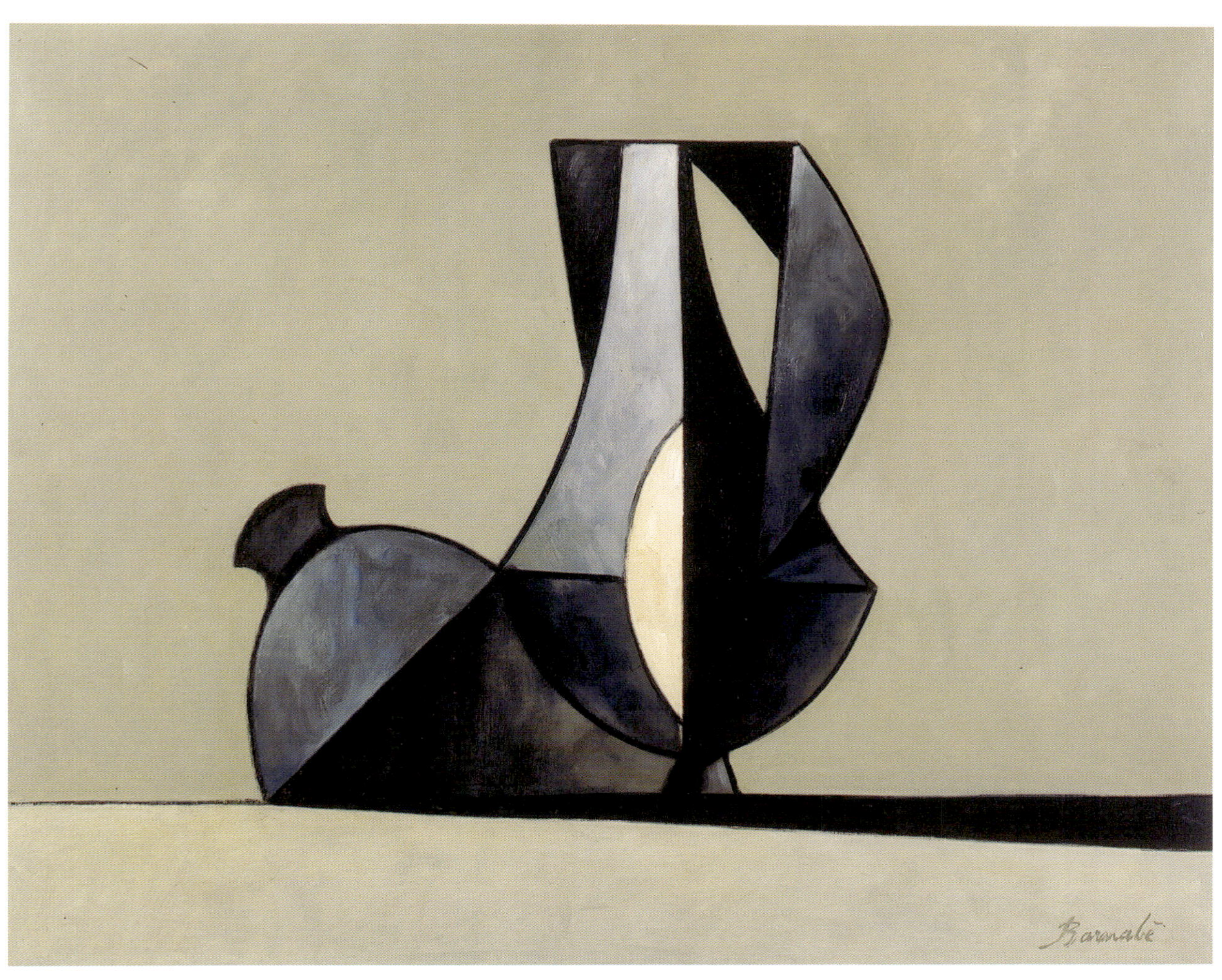

13. ***Natura morta,*** 1951
    Still Life

    Oil on canvas
    77 x 112 cm.; 30 1/2 x 44 inches
    Signed and dated, upper right

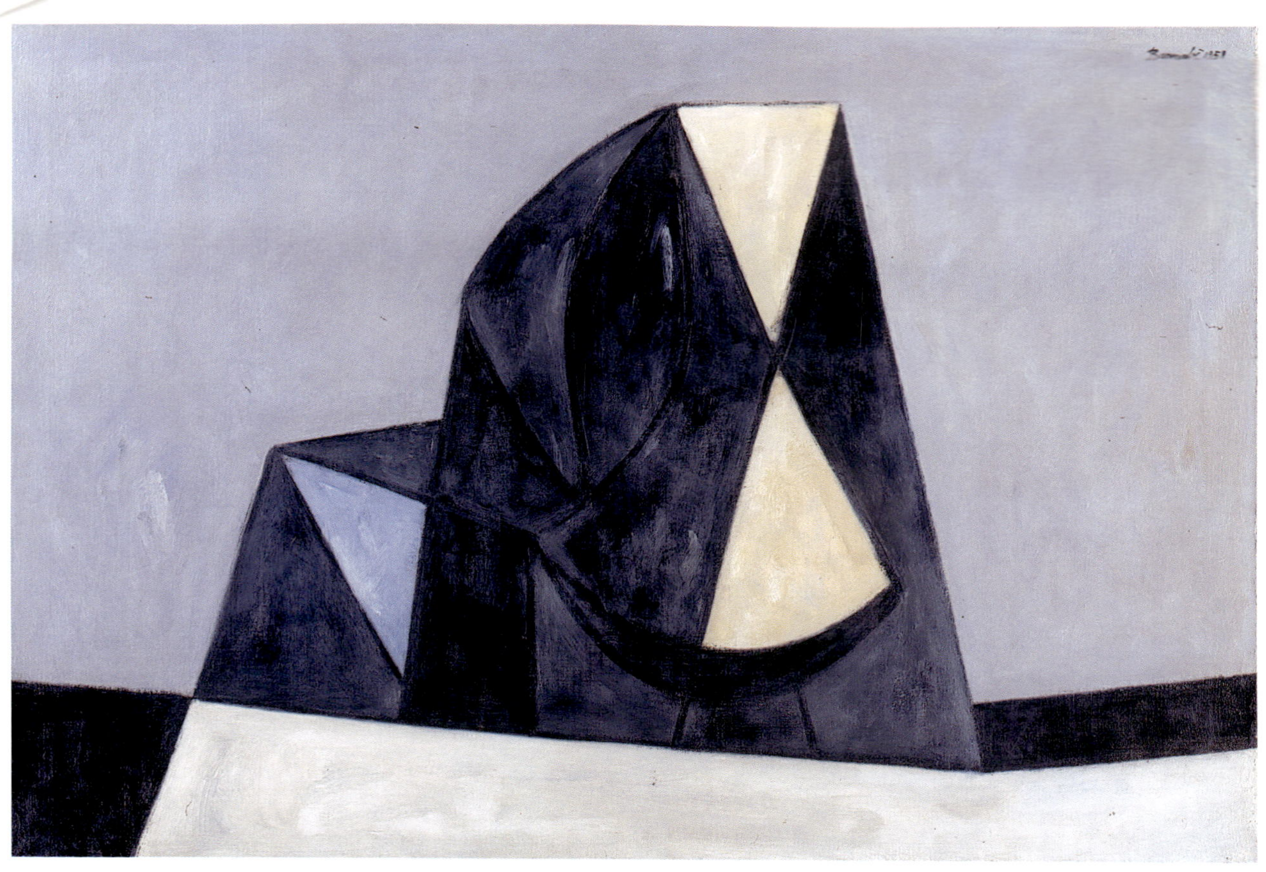

14. *Figura seduta, fondo blu* , about 1952
   Sitting Figure: Blue background

   Oil on canvas
   121 x 75.5 cm.; 47 1/2 x 29 3/4 inches
   Signed, upper right

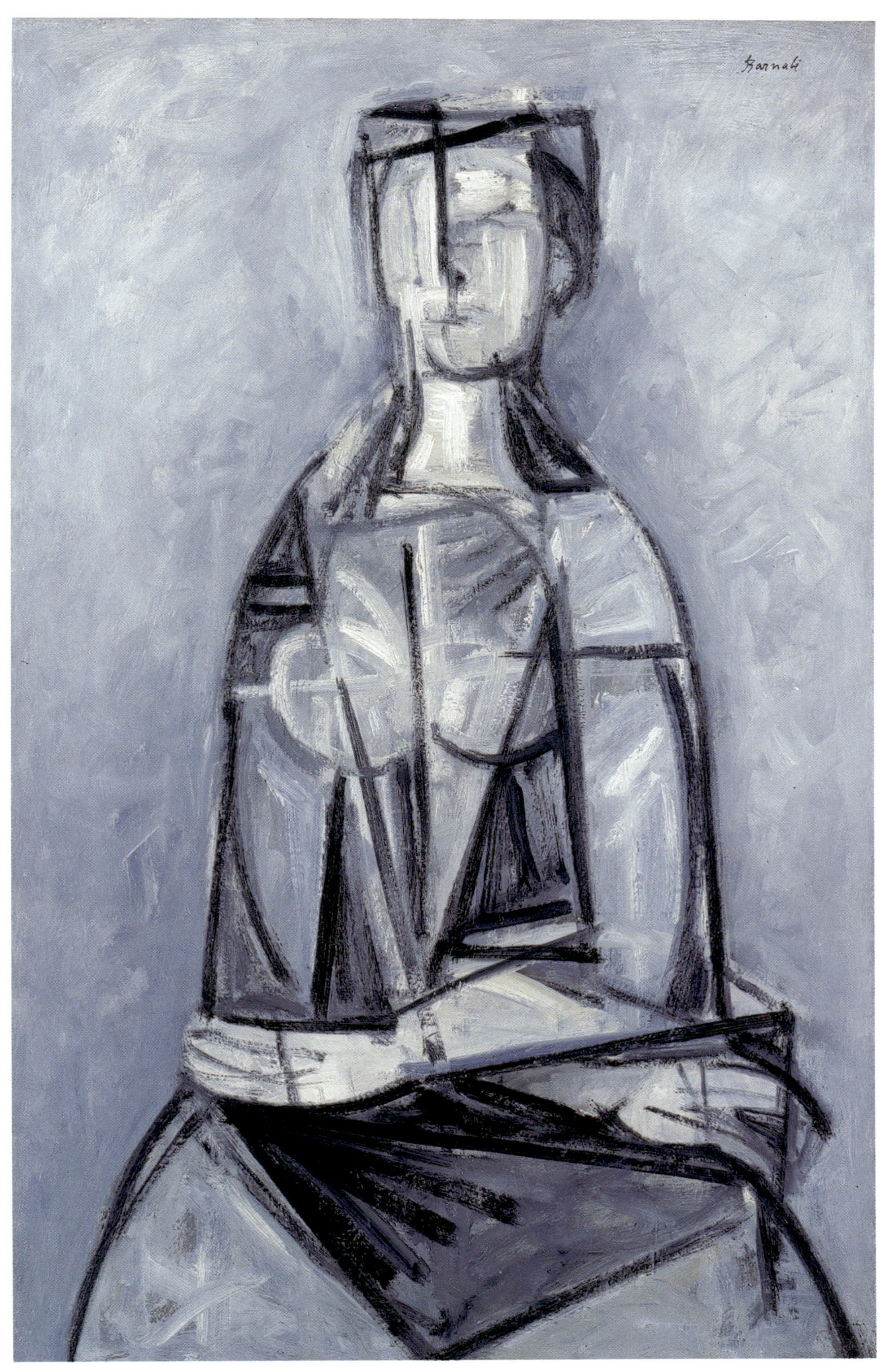

Barnati

15. ***Paesaggio***, 1952
    Landscape

    Oil on canvas
    85 x 100 cm.; 33 1/2 x 39 3/8 inches
    Signed and dated, lower right

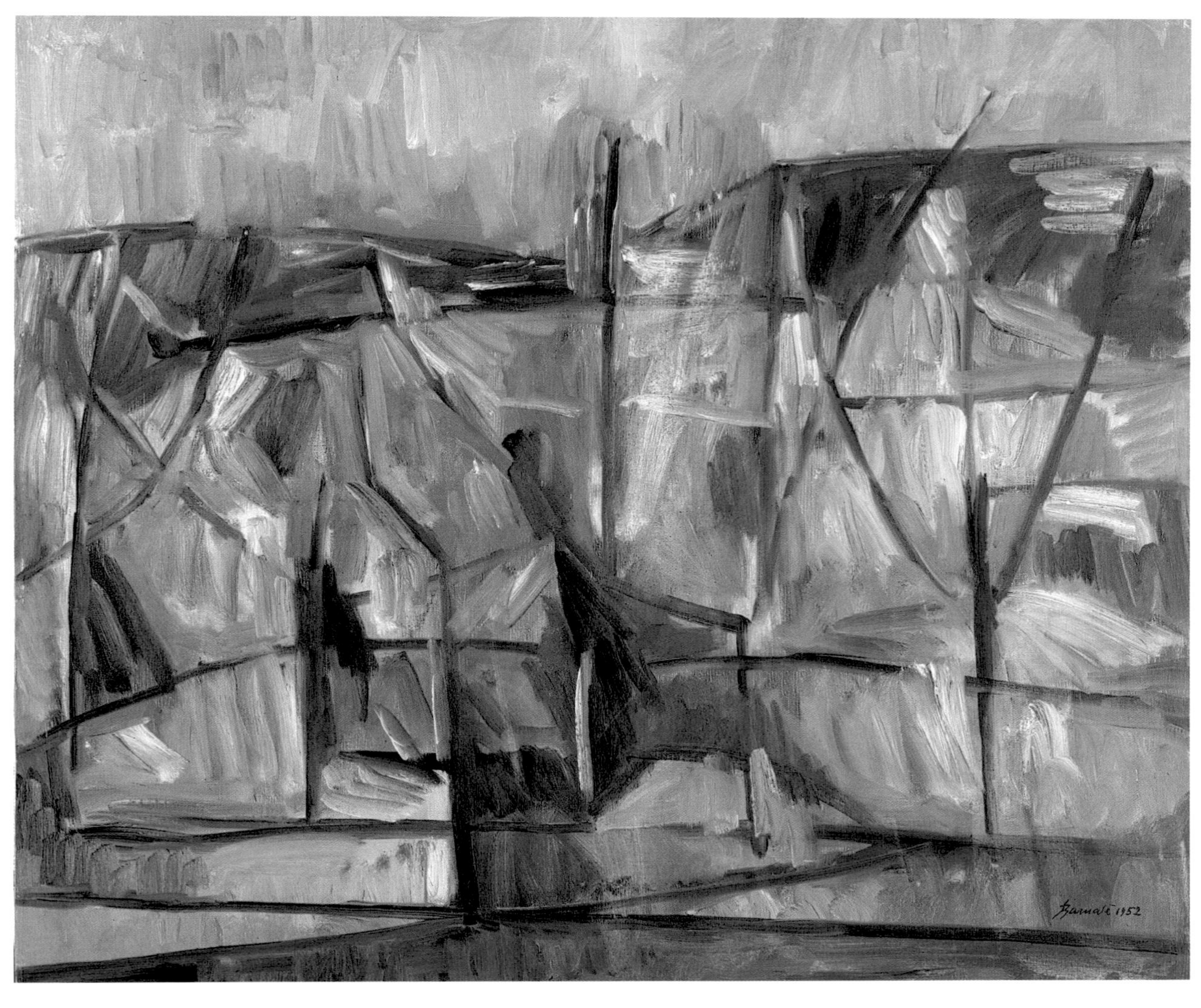

16. ***Cattedrale,*** about 1952
Cathedral

Oil on canvas
91 x 143 cm.; 36 x 55 1/2 inches
Titled on verso

Provenance:
The estate of the artist

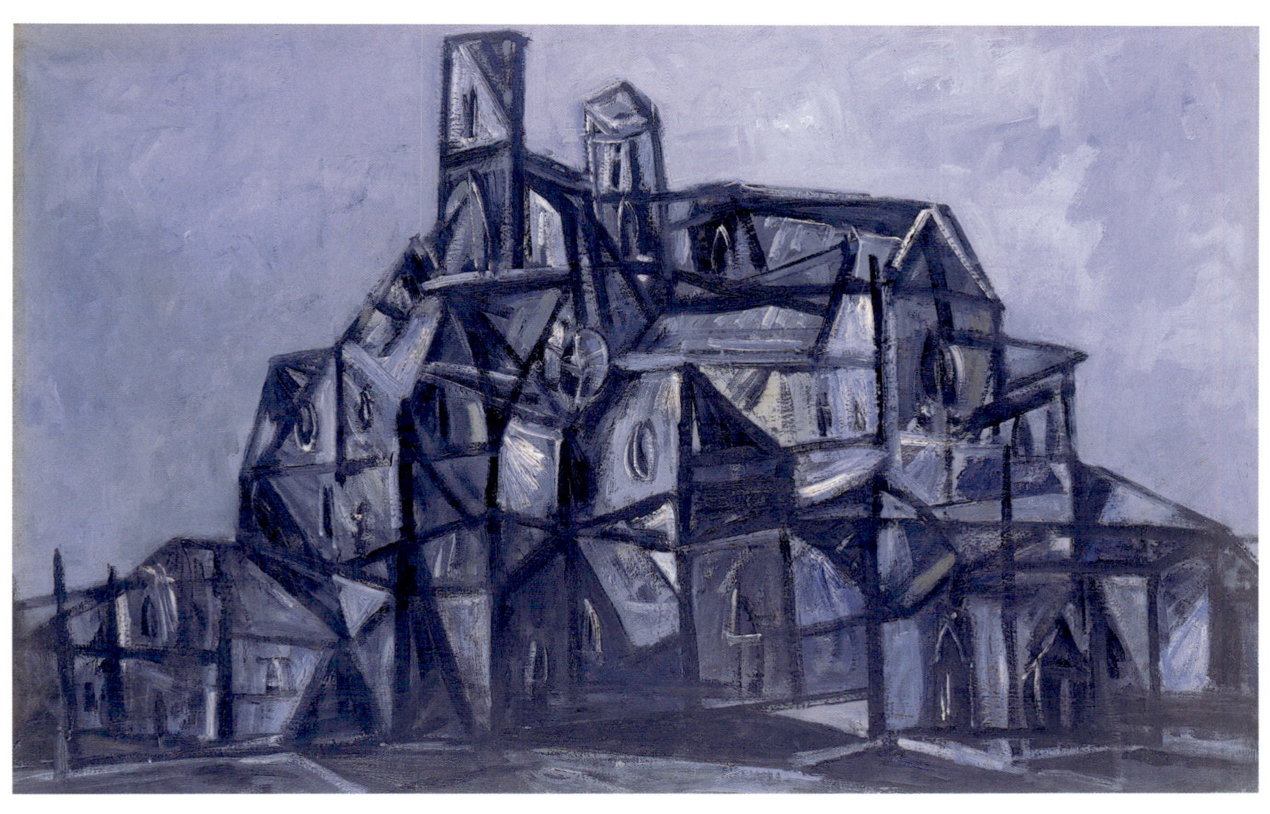

17. ***Barche in un porto,*** about 1952
   Boats in a Harbor

   Oil on canvas
   70.5 x 100 cm.; 28 x 39 1/4 inches
   Signed, lower left

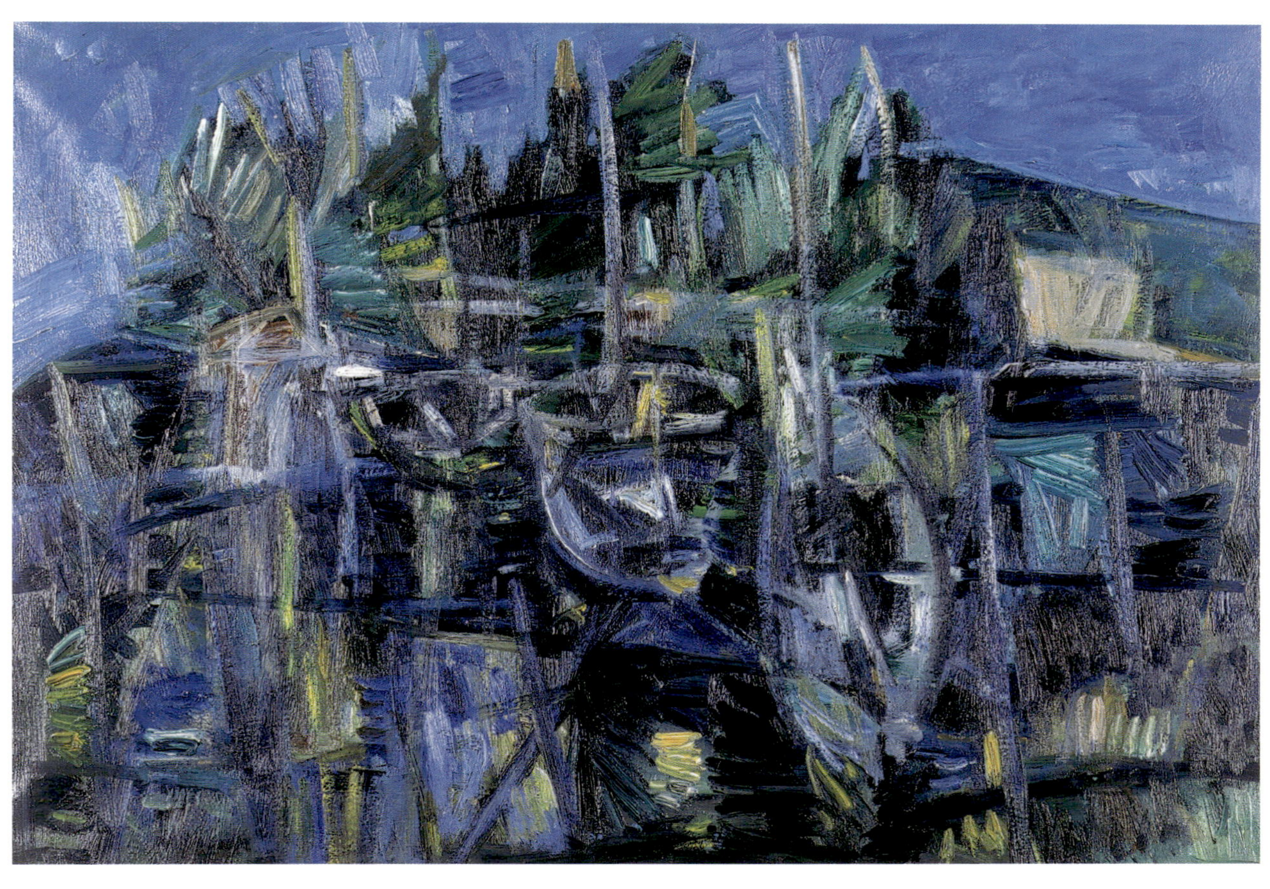

18. ***La luna a Portese,*** 1952-1953
Moonlight in Portese

Oil on canvas
75.5 x 121 cm.; 29 3/4 x 41 1/2 inches
Signed, dated and titled, lower left

Note:
1. This work appears to be dated "1955". If so, this certainly refers to a date when Barnabè either
    sold or gave away this painting. The painting itself corresponds to a series of other works
    executed by Barnabè in 1952 or 1953. For comparable Barnabè landscapes around this date,
    see plate no. 17 from about 1952 and plate nos. 21, 22 and 23 from about 1953.
2. Barnabè painted this work in Portese, probably in either the summer of 1952 or 1953. Portese
    is a tiny fishing village on Lago di Garda, in the mountains to the north of Bologna. In 1932,
    the Verona artist, Adriano Bogoni, who loved the beauty of Garda, decided to establish there
    una scuola di pittura all'aperto ("a school of open-air painting"). Bogoni's choice of
    Portese was not haphazard since he first explored all other possibilities around the Lago di
    Garda. He found Portese to be such an enchanting *paradiso* that he dedicated a poem to
    the little harbor, a poem stating that Sicily, Napoli and Capri are each *bella*, but that *ma
    Portese è miglior*e ("my Portese is the most beautiful").

    > Ed è con vero rammarico che, quando le ultime foglie ingiallite cadono lentamente,
    > farfalleggiando nell'aria un ultimo saluto al sole che va raffreddandosi, l'ospite
    > lascia questi luogho di paradiso per ritornare nel turbine della vita cittadina.

    > Conosco bene la Sicilia: bella!
    > Conosco bene Napoli: bella!
    > Conosco bene Capri: bella!
    > Ma Portese è migliore.

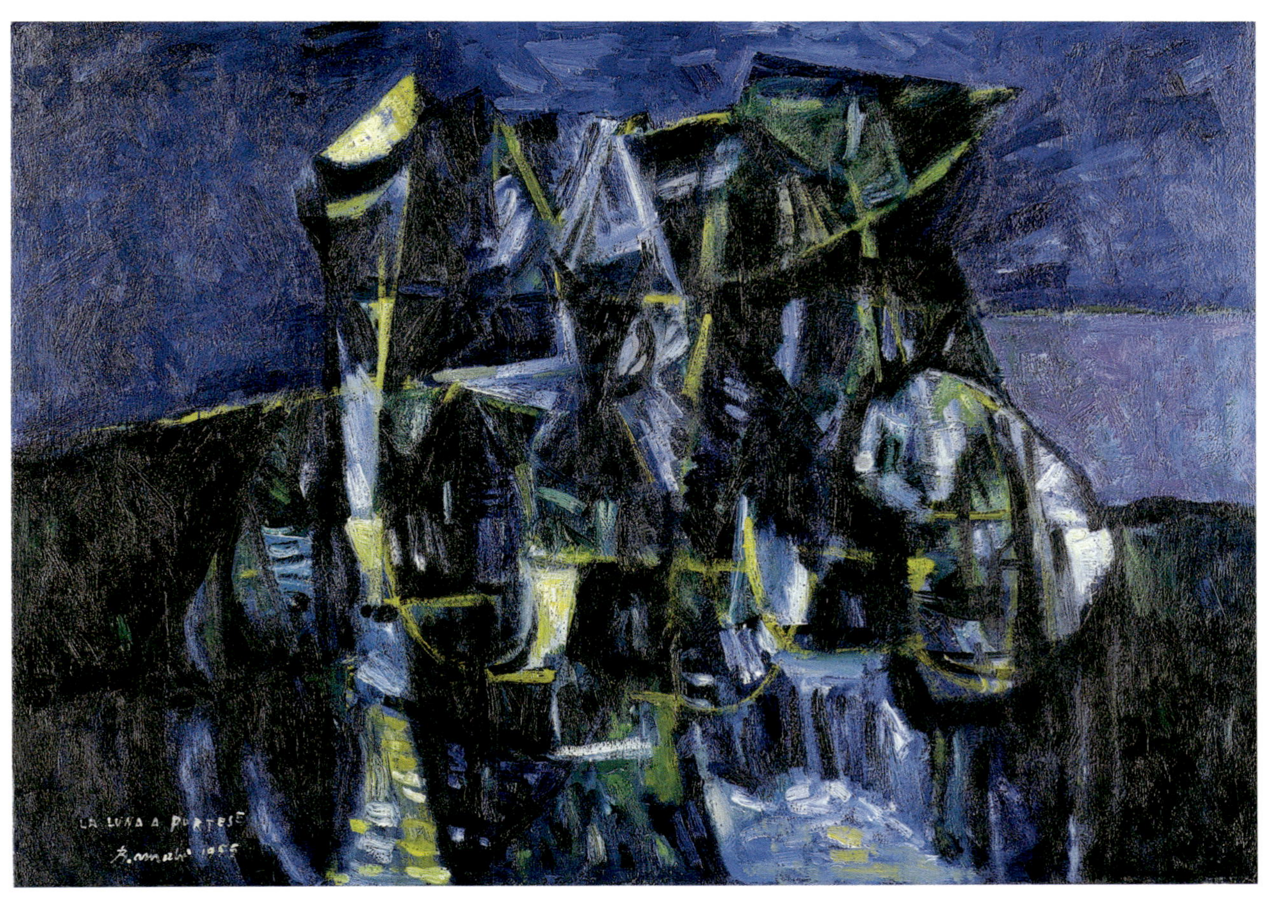
LA LUNA A PORTESE

19. ***Donna con crocchia***, 1952
Woman with Chignon

Oil on canvas
100 x 84.5 cm.; 39 3/4 x 34 inches
Signed and dated, upper right

Verso:
Counter-signed and dated

Collection:
Lee B. and Norma Stern

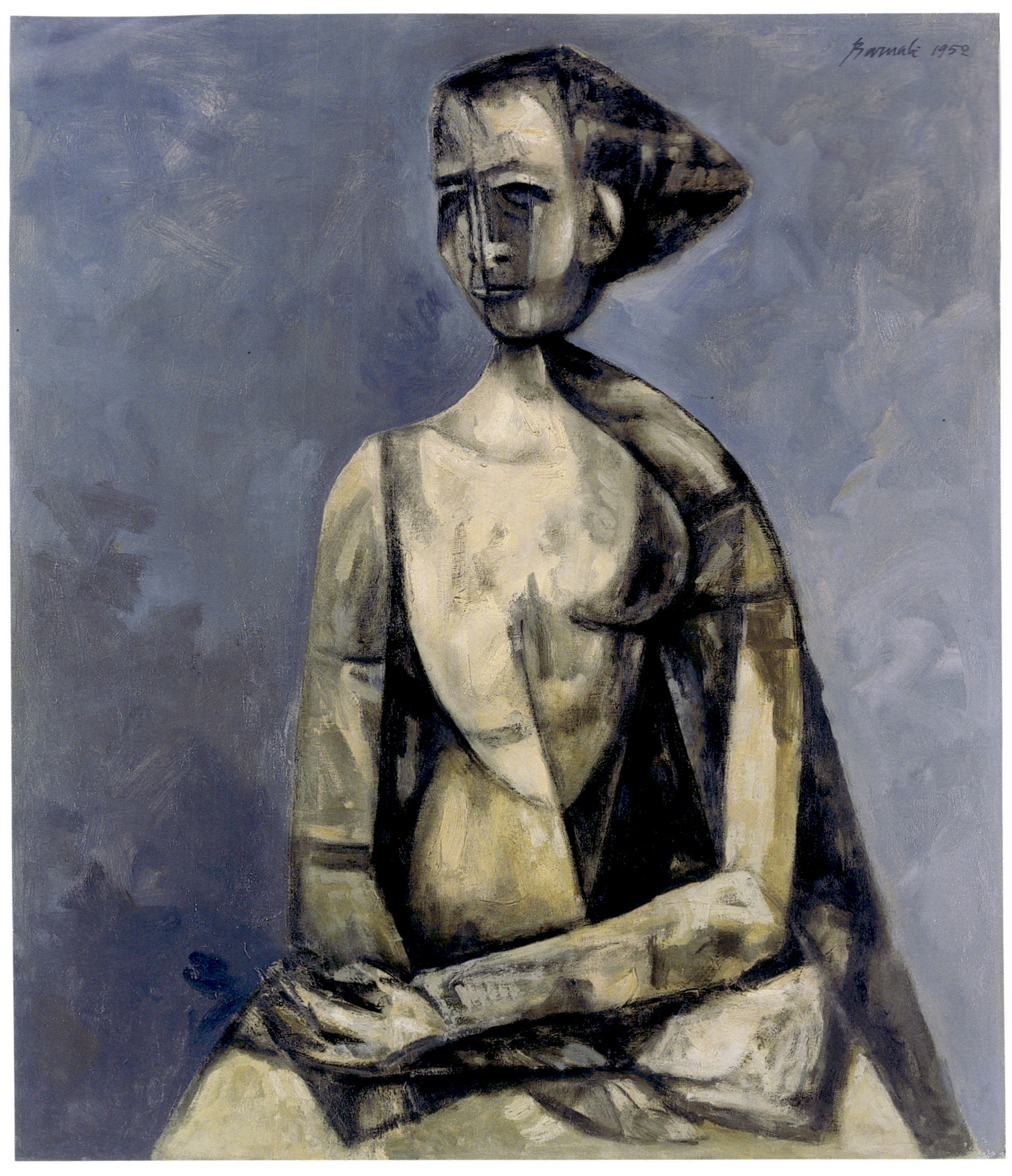

Bernáth 1952

20. *Ragazza seduta,* 1952
   Young Girl Sitting

   Oil on canvas
   100 x 81 cm.; 39 12/4 x 32 inches
   Signed and dated, upper right

   Collection:
   Amod and Dershi Saxena

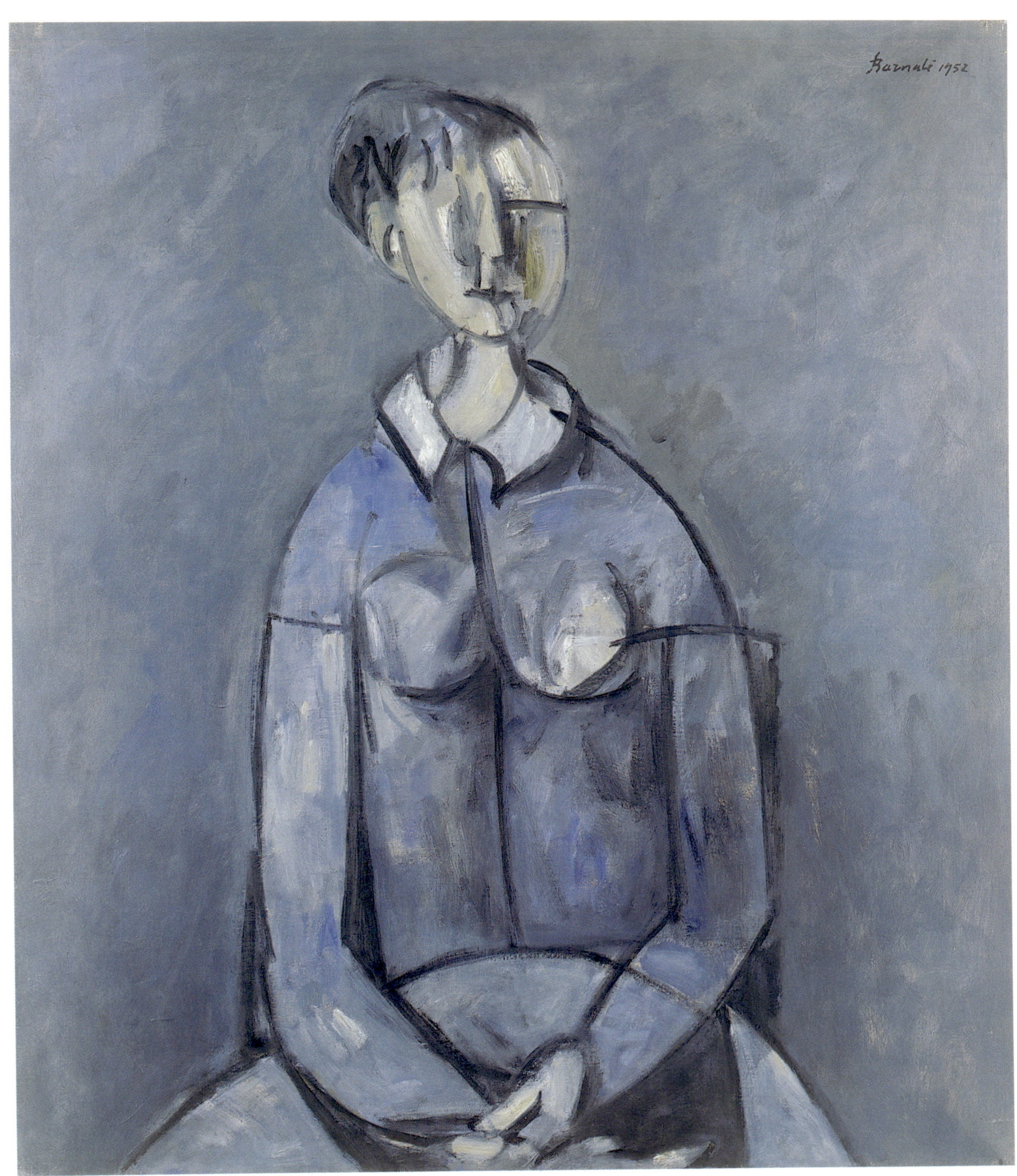

21. ***Paesaggio blu,*** 1953
Landscape in Blue

Mixed media on paper
39.4 x 58.4 cm.; 15 1/2 x 23 inches
Signed and dated, lower right

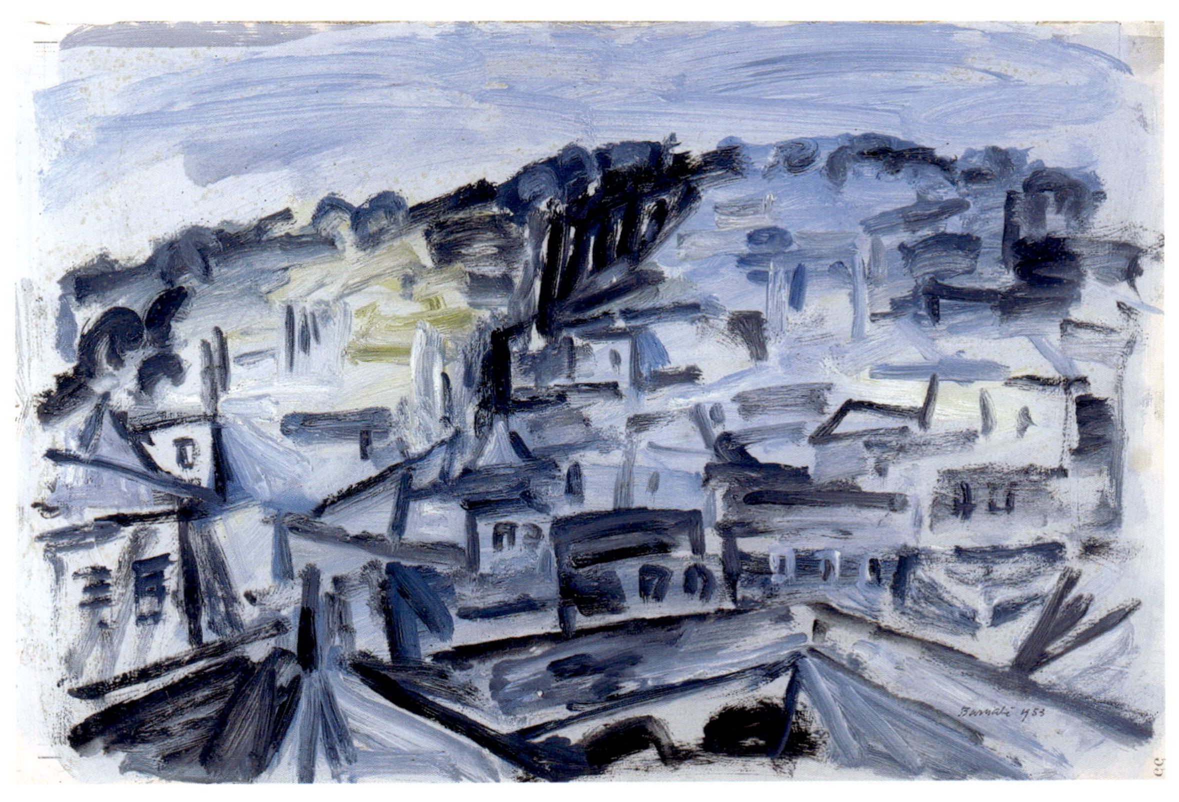

22. ***Scena del fiume***, 1953
River Scene

Watercolor and ink on ledger paper
39.4 x 55.9 cm.; 15 x 21 5/8 inches
Signed and dated, lower right

23. ***Paesaggio***, 1953
Landscape

Watercolor and ink on ledger paper
39.4 x 55.9 cm.; 15 x 21 5/8 inches
Signed and dated, lower right

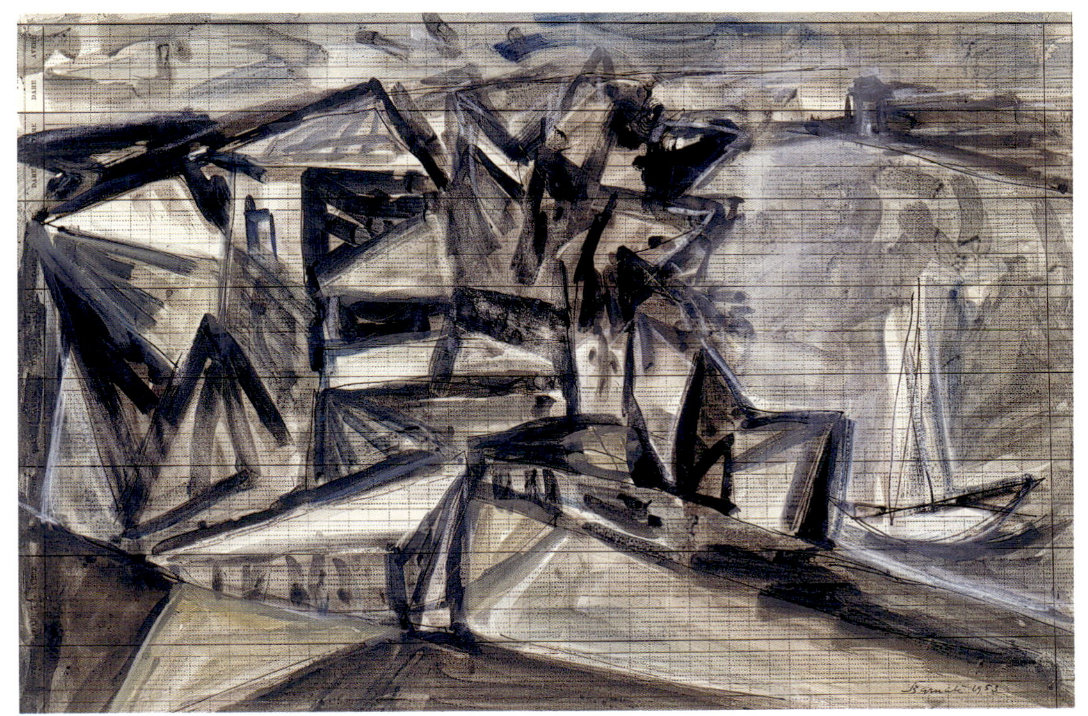

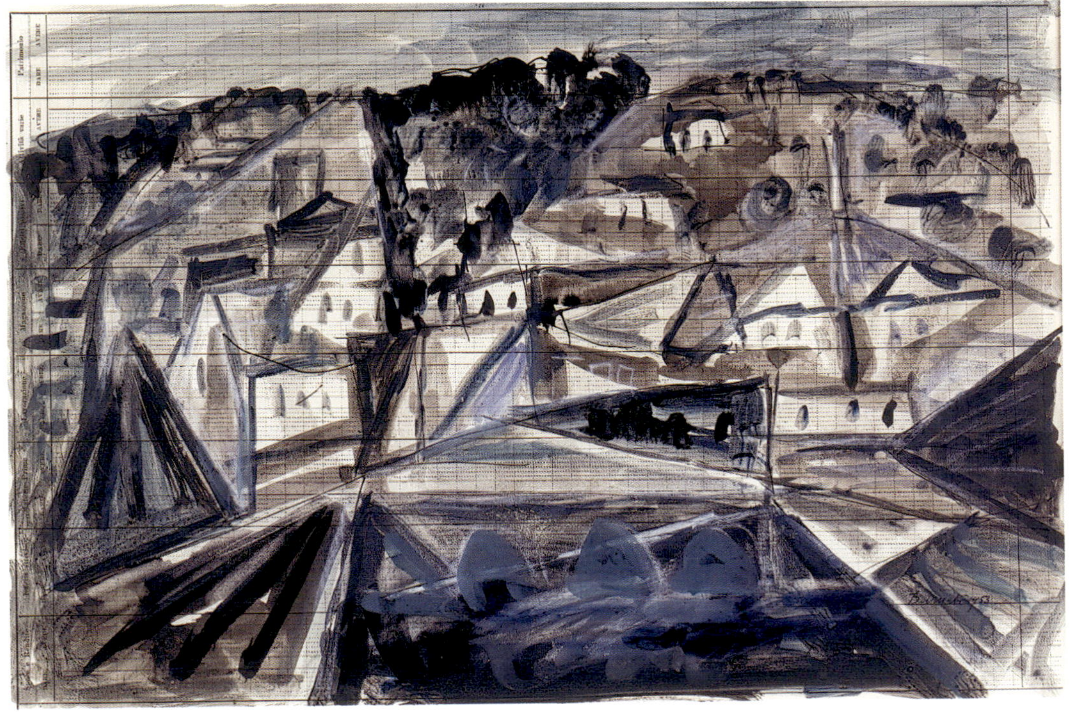

24. ***Figura seduta, fondo marrone,*** about 1953
Sitting Figure: Brown Background

Oil on canvas
100 x 85 cm.; 39 1/2 x 33 3/8 inches
Signed, upper right

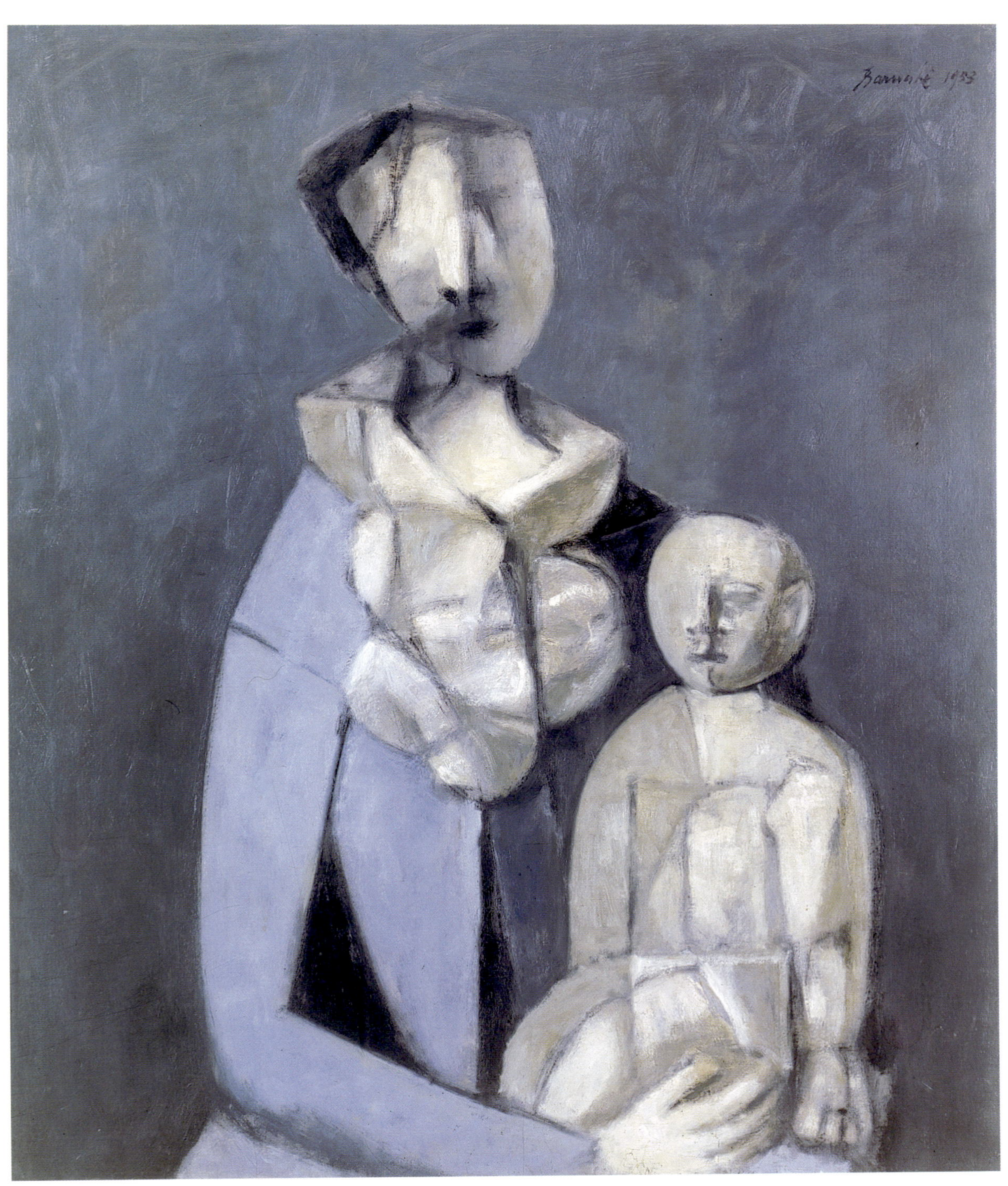

26. ***Due figure sedute ad un tavolo,*** about 1954
Two Figures Seated at a Table

Oil on canvas
65 x 81 cm.; 25 1/2 x 31 3/4 inches
Signed, lower right

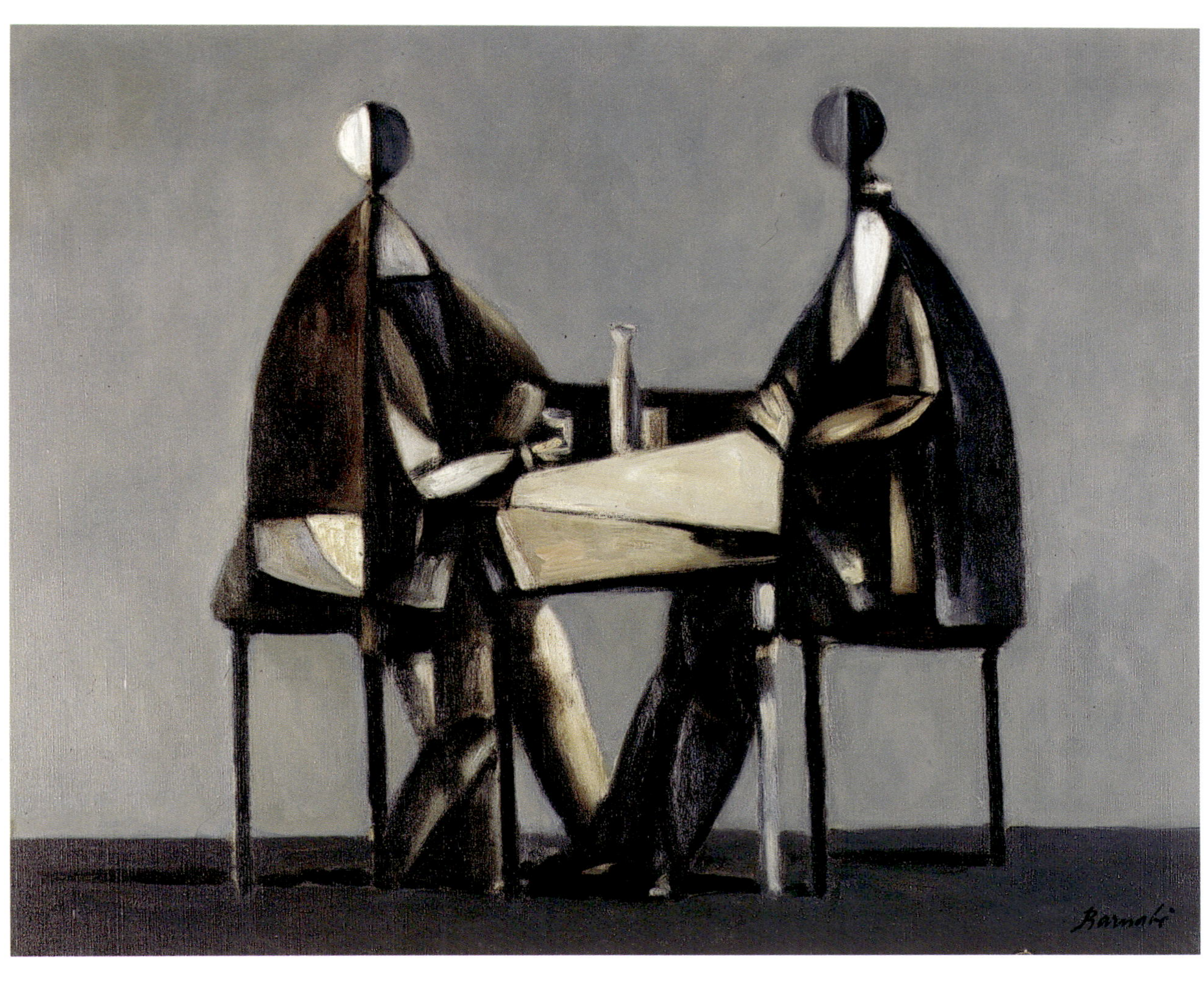

27. ***Pittore e modella,*** about 1954
Painter and model

Oil on canvas
38.8 x 61.6 cm; 15 1/8 x 24 1/4 inches
Signed, lower right

28. ***Pittore e modella,*** about 1954
Painter and model

Oil on canvas
18.5 x 29.2 cm.; 7 3/16 x 11 1/2 inches
Signed, lower right

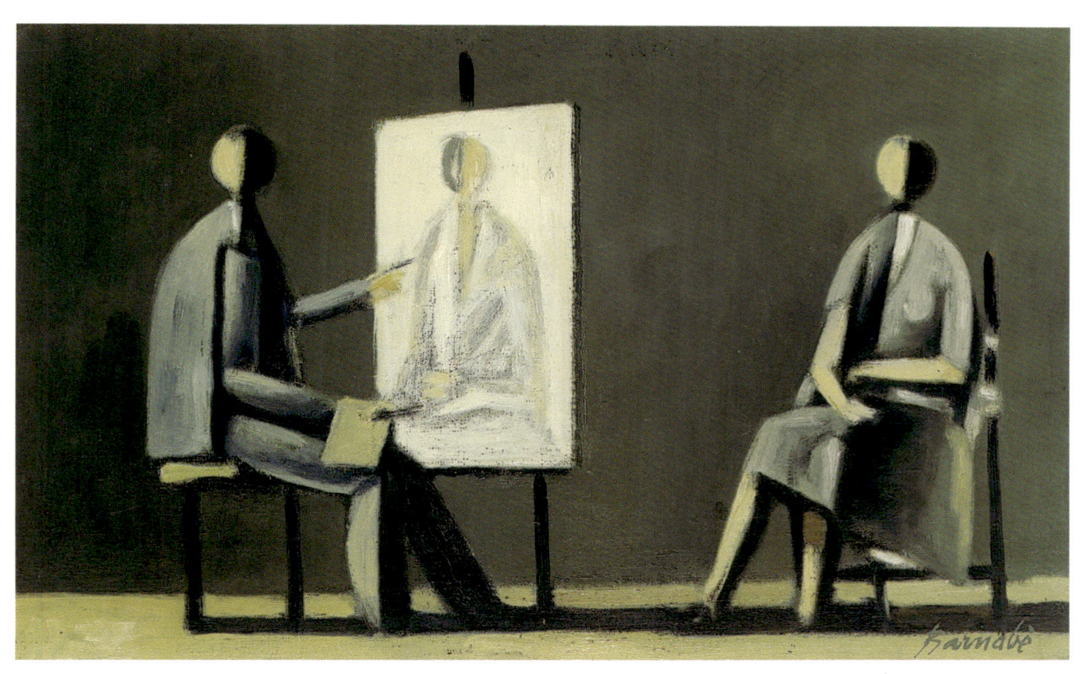

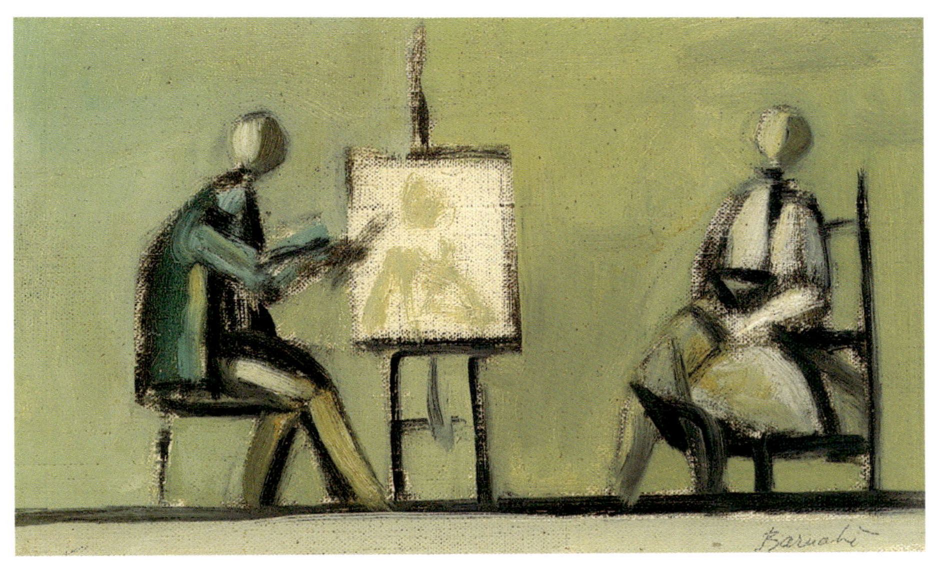

29. **_Due caraffe_**, about 1954
   Two Decanters

   Oil on canvas
   81 x 100 cm.; 32 x 39 1/4 inches
   Signed, lower right

30. **_Due caraffe,_** about 1954
   Two Decanters

   Charcoal and gouache
   50.8 x 83.2 cm.; 20 x 32 3/4 inches
   Signed in pencil, lower right

   (reproduced on page 14)

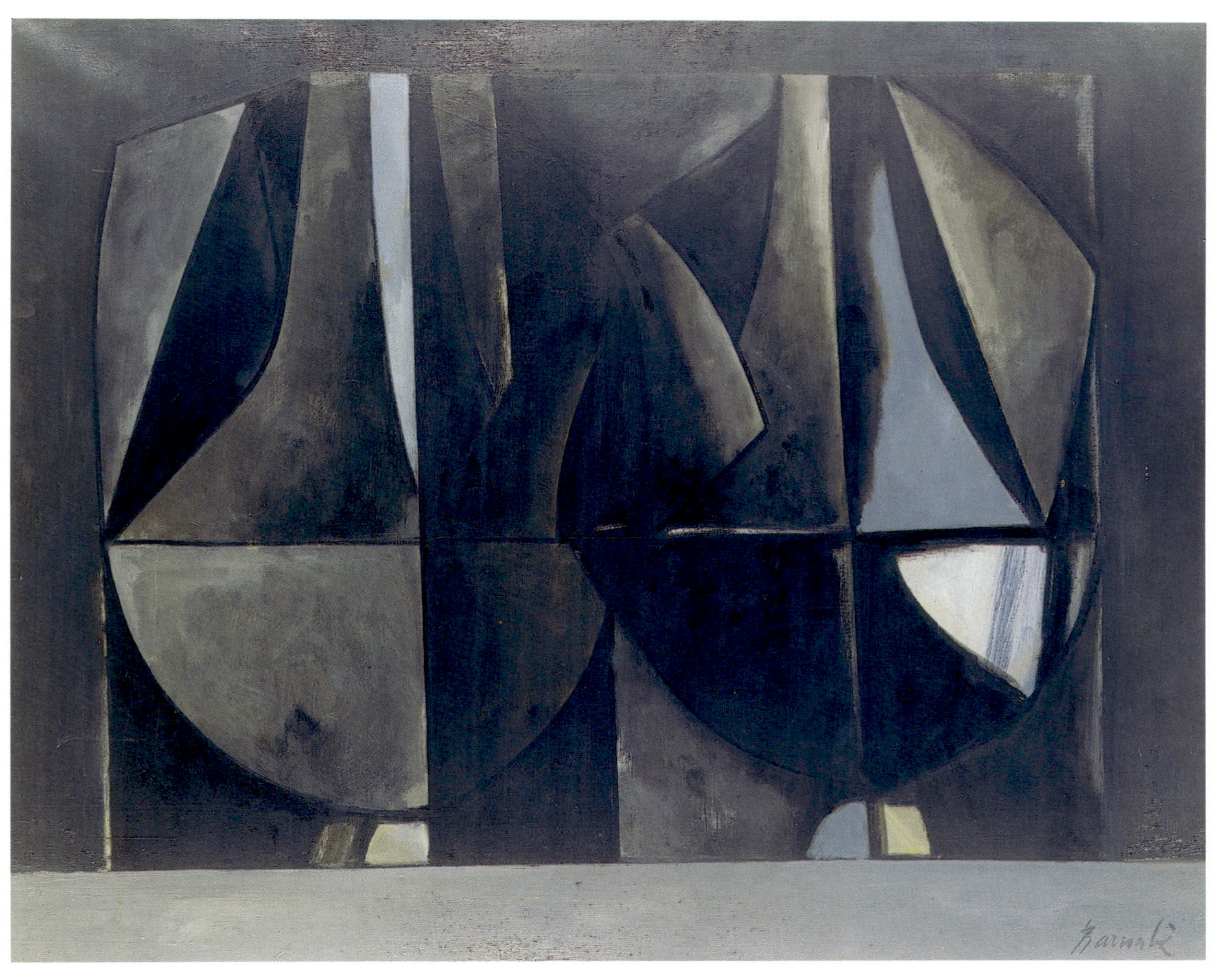

31. ***Pescatori,*** about 1955
Fishermen

Charcoal and gouache
50.8 x 63.5cm.; 20 x 25 inches
Signed, lower right

32. ***Caffettiera***, about 1954
Coffee Pot

Gouache
47.6 x 70.5 cm.; 18 3/4 x 27 3/4 inches
Signed, lower right

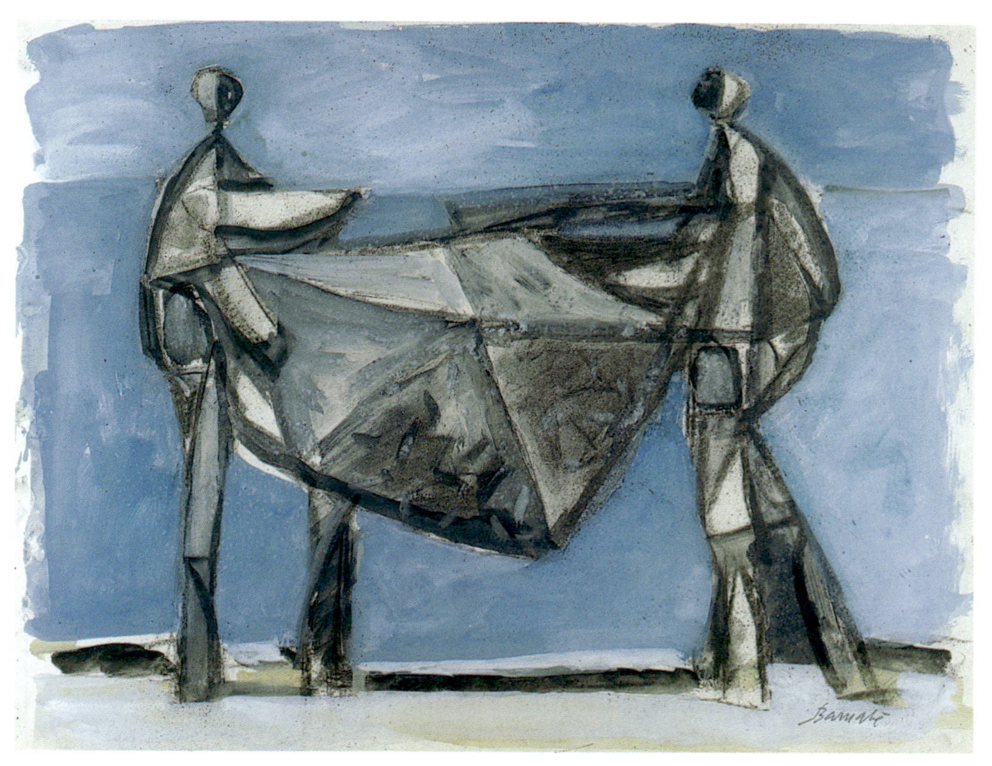

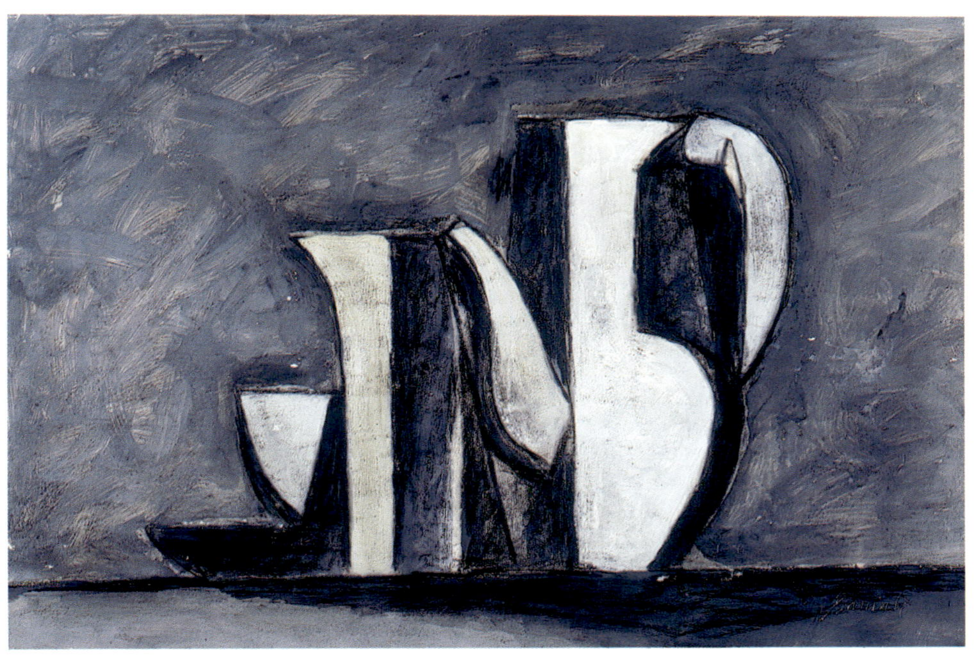

33. ***Due suore***, 1954
Two Nuns

Oil on canvas
114 x 145 cm.; 45 x 57 1/4 inches
Signed

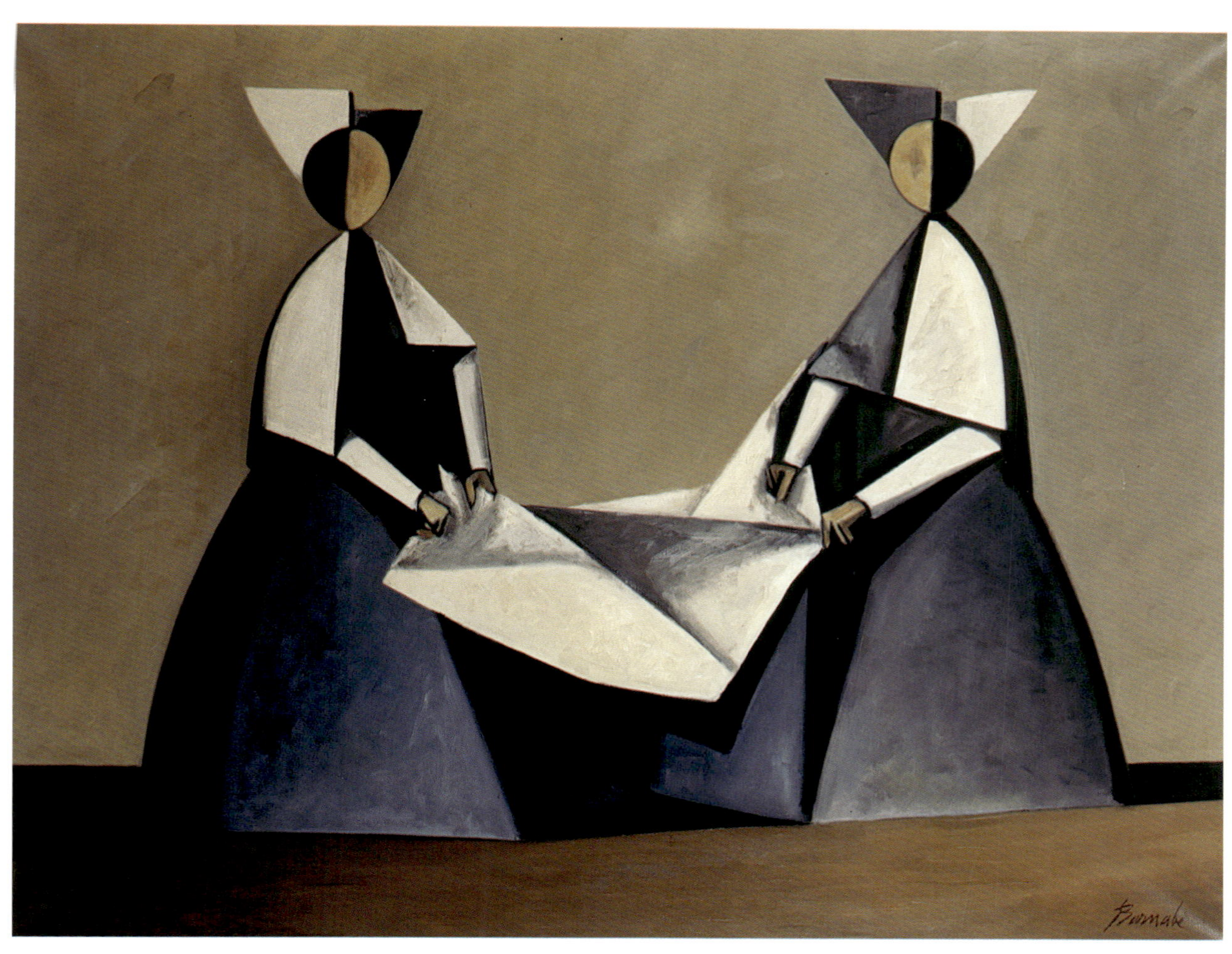

34. *Pierrot*, about 1955
   Pierrot

   Charcoal and gouache
   73.7 x 55.9 cm.; 29 x 22 inches
   Signed, lower right

35. *Due suore*, 1955
   Two Nuns

   Pencil
   49.5 x 64.1cm.; 19 1/2 x 25 1/4 inches
   Signed and dated, lower right

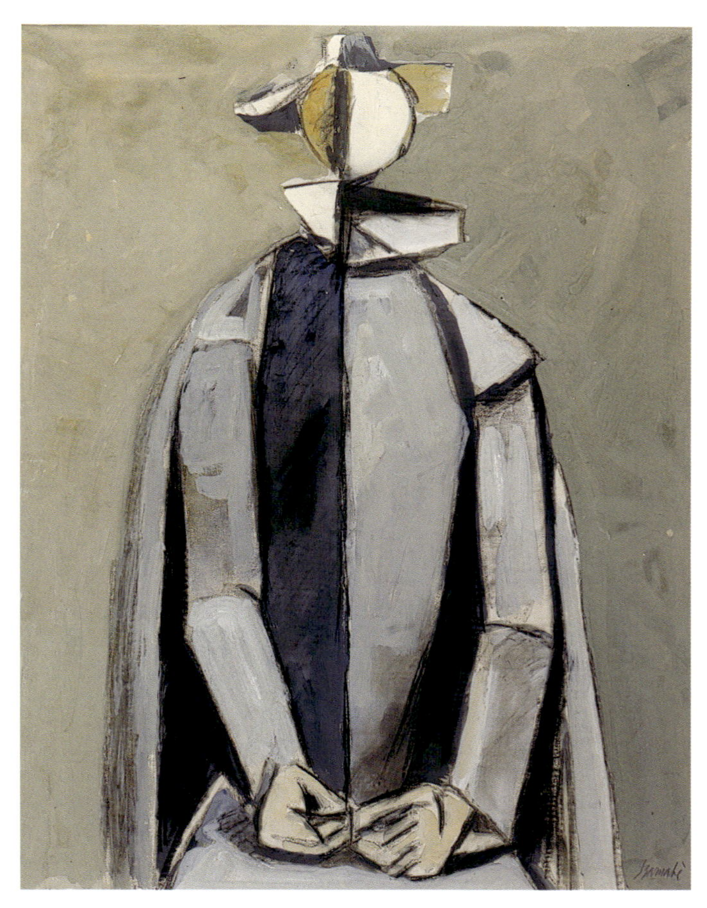

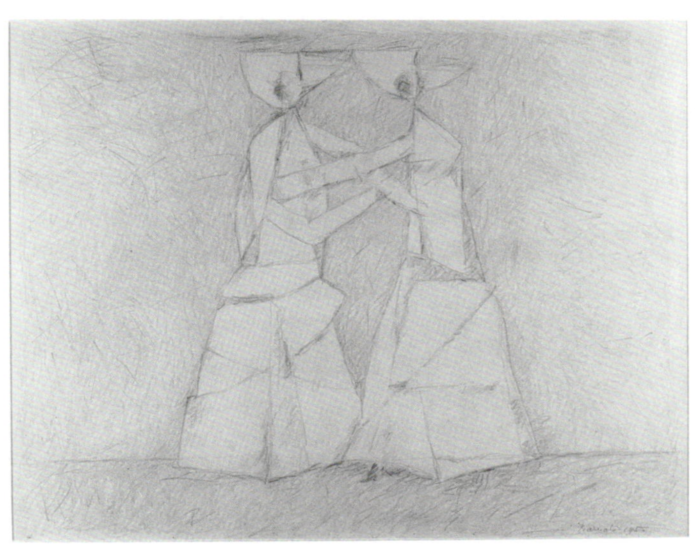

36. ***Suora***, about 1955
Nun

Pencil and gouache
69.9 x 41.3 cm.; 27 1/2 x 16 1/4 inches
Signed, lower right

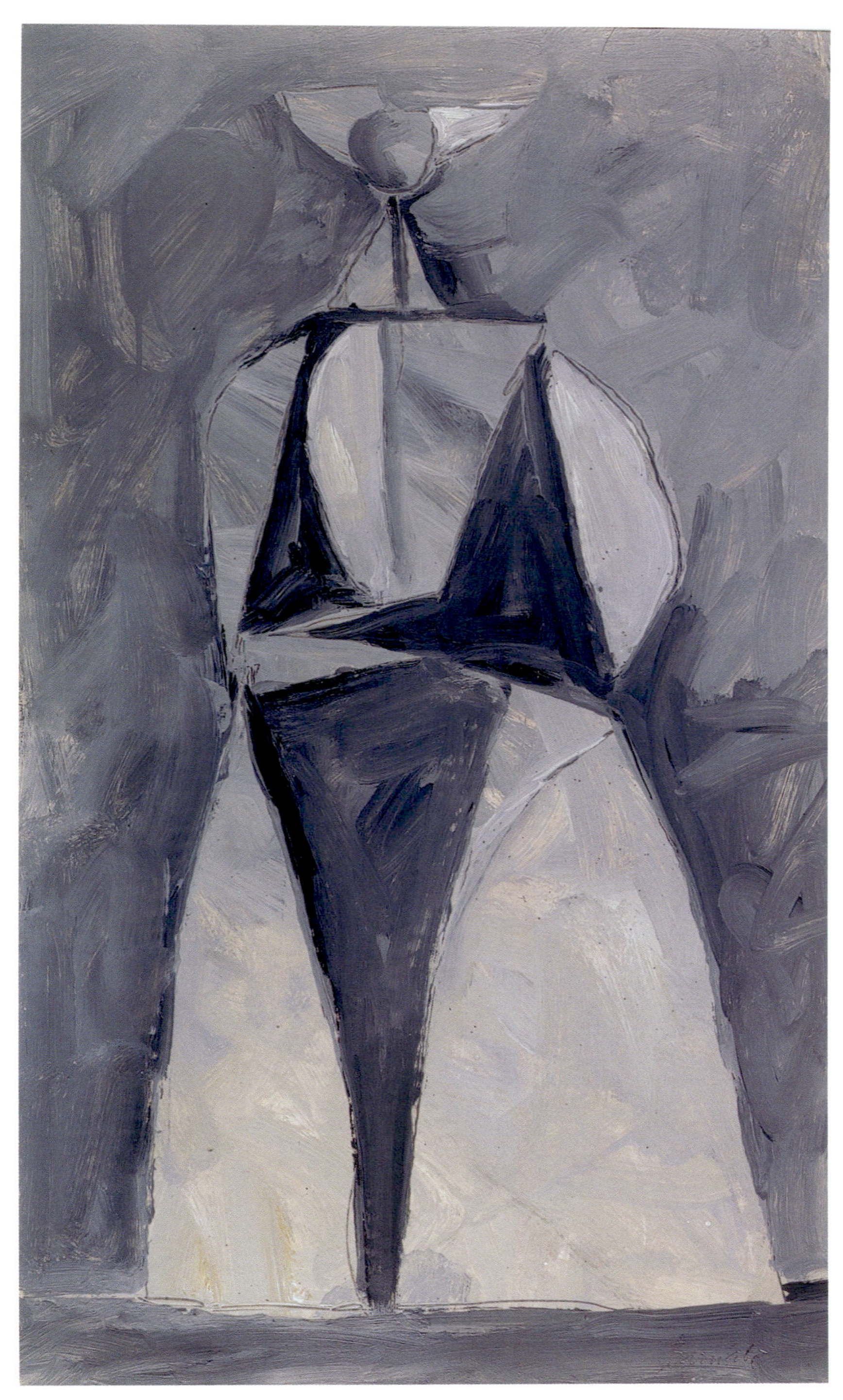

37. *Caraffa con macinino del caffé*, about 1955
   Pitcher with Coffee-Maker

   Oil on canvas
   58.5 x 72.5 cm.; 23 x 28 1/2 inches
   Signed, lower right

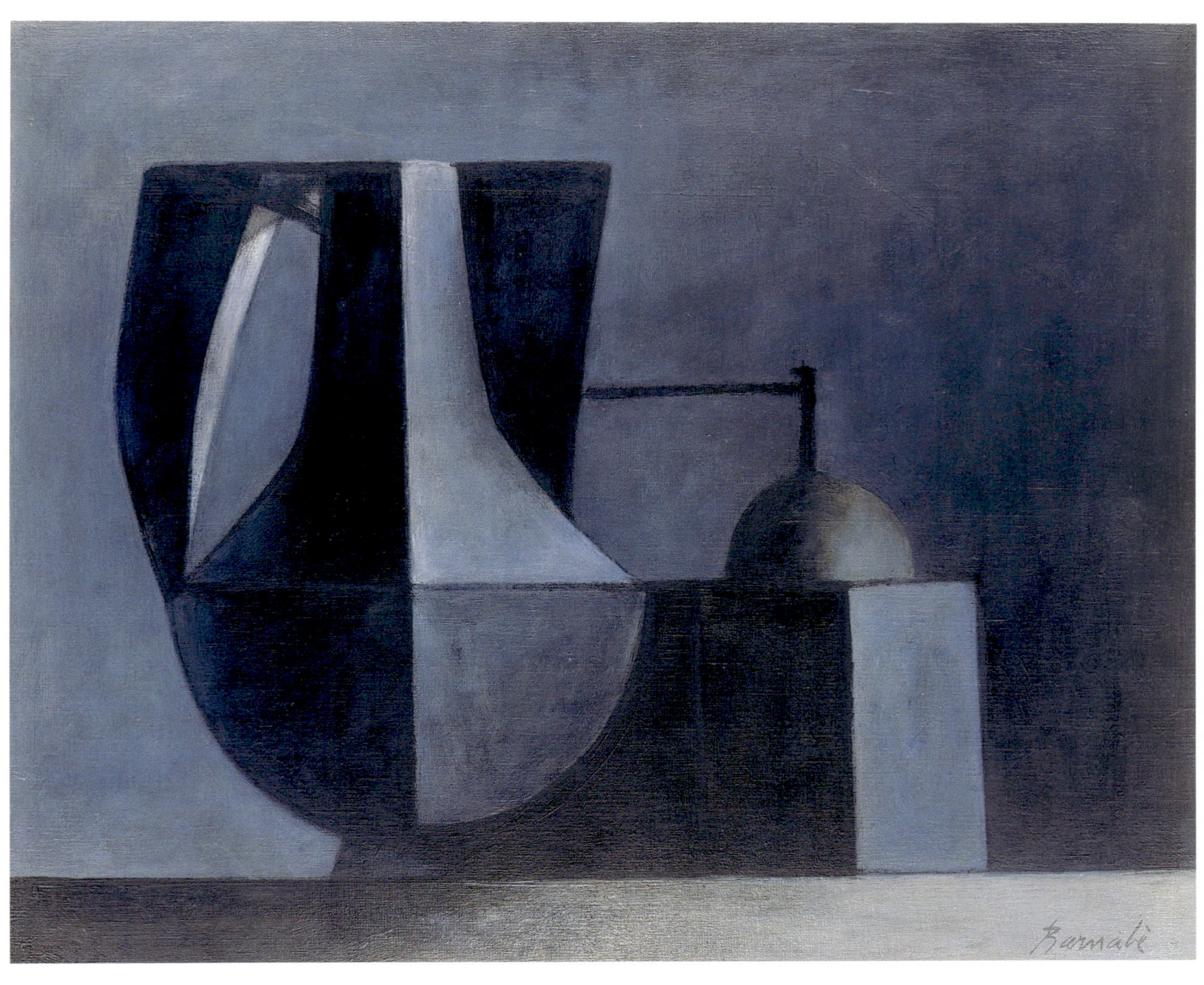

Barnabé

38. *Natura morta,* about 1955-56
    Still Life

    Oil on canvas
    38.5 x 54 cm.; 15 x 21 3/4 inches
    Signed, lower right

38a. *Mazzo di fiori blu e grigio*, about 1955
    Bouquet in Blue and Gray

    Charcoal and gouache
    80 x 60 cm.; 24 x 18 inches
    Signed, lower right

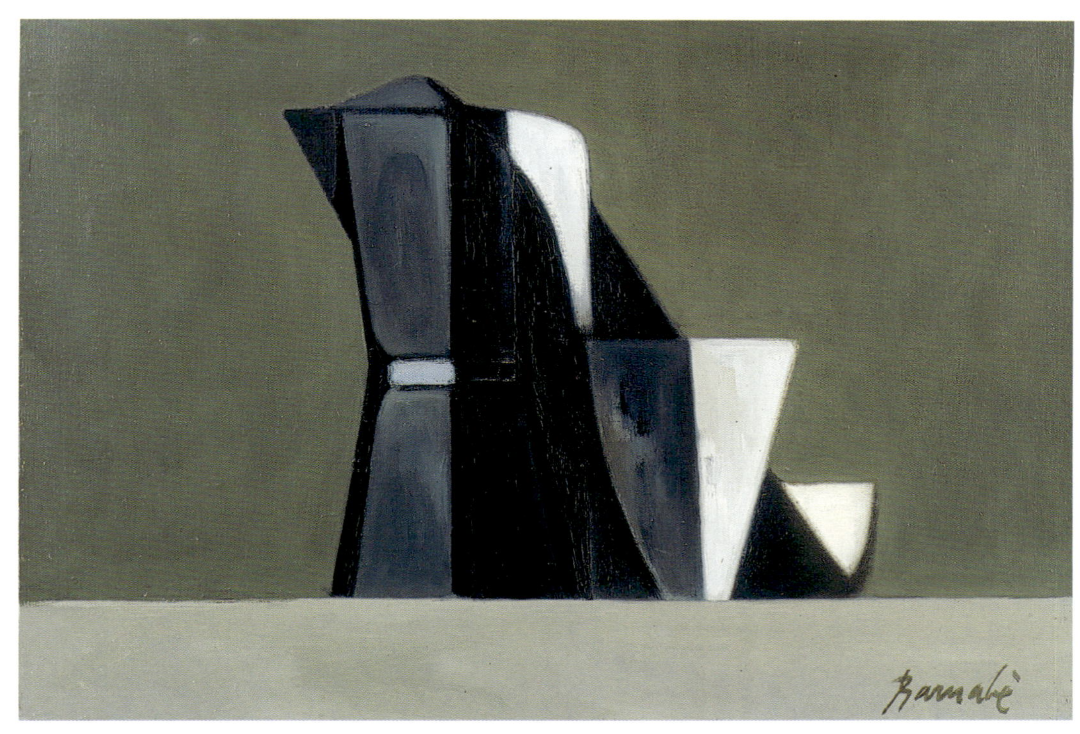

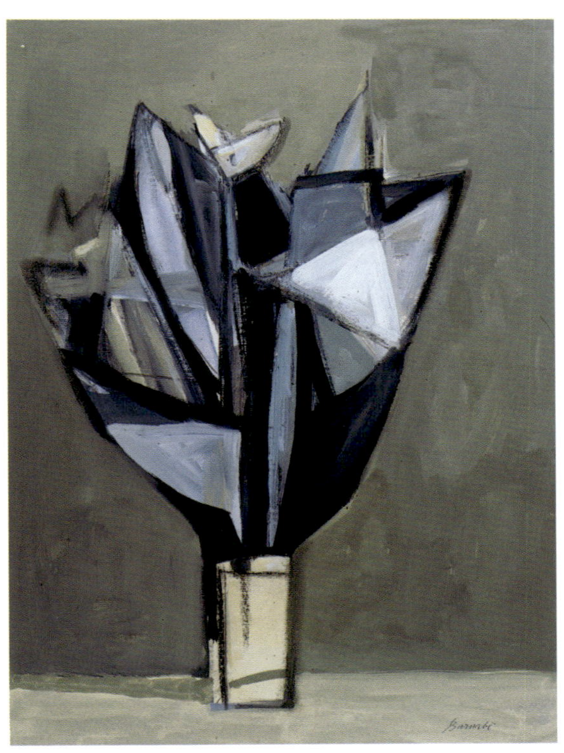

39. ***Tre suore,*** about 1956
Three Nuns

Oil on canvas
54 x 81 cm.; 21 1/4 x 31 1/2 inches
Signed, lower right

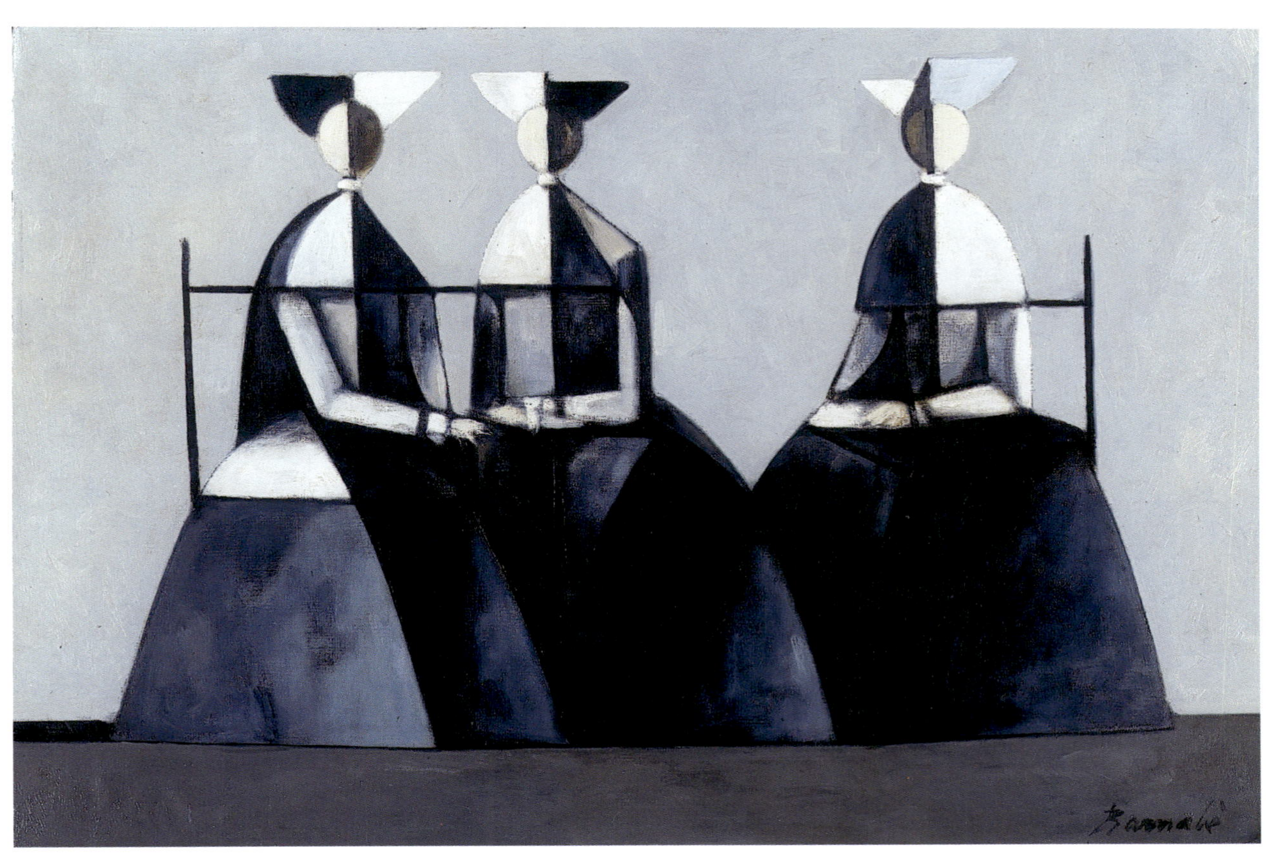

40. ***Mazzo di fiori***, about 1956
Bouquet

Oil on canvas
92 x 60 cm.; 36 1/4 x 23 1/2 inches
Signed, lower right

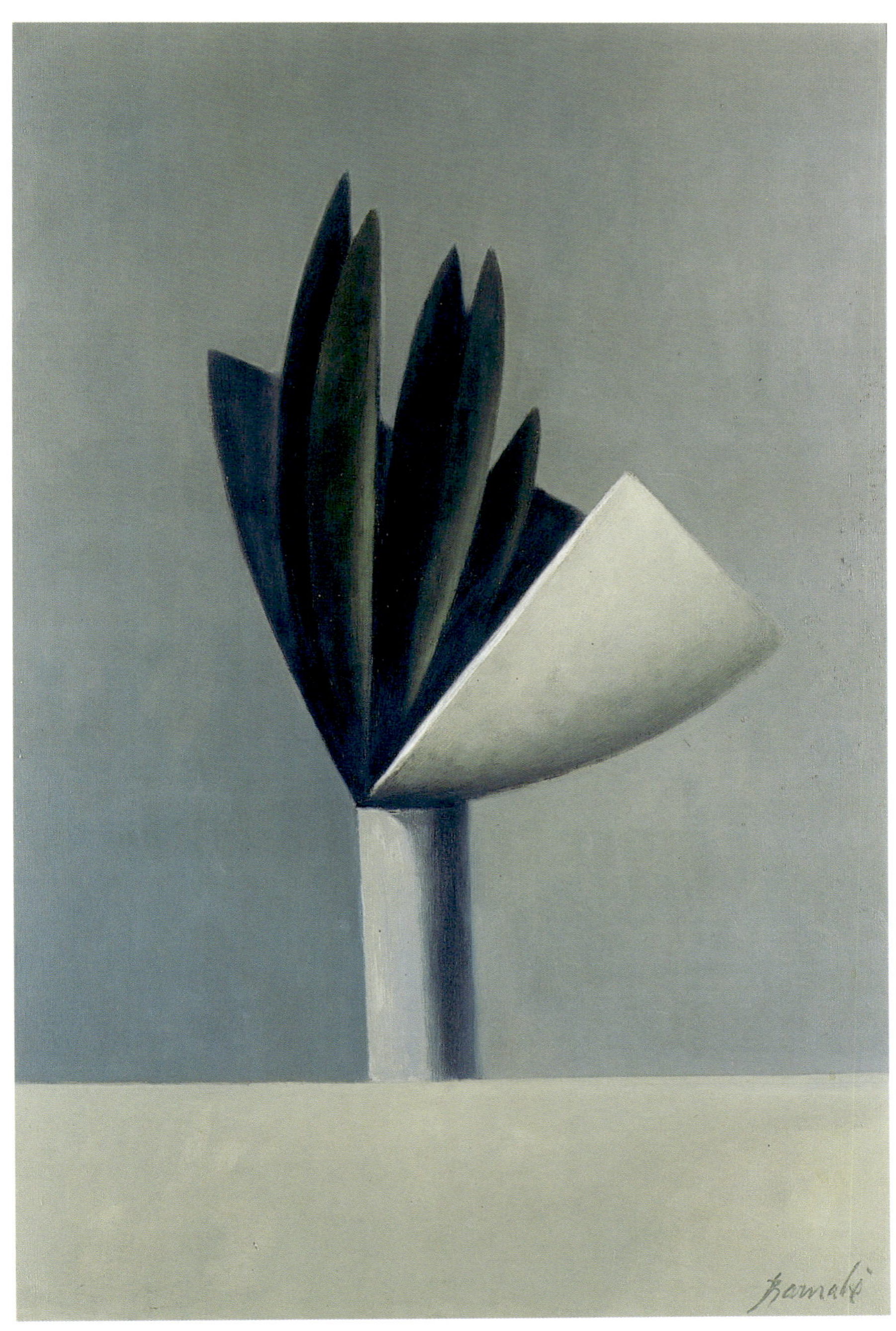

41. ***San Sebastiano,*** about 1956
Saint Sebastian

Oil on canvas
162 x 97.2 cm.; 63 7/8 x 38 1/4 inches
Signed, lower right

42. ***Pierrot****, about1956
Pierrot

Oil on canvas
61 x 38 cm.; 24 x 15 inches
Signed, lower right

(reproduced on page15)

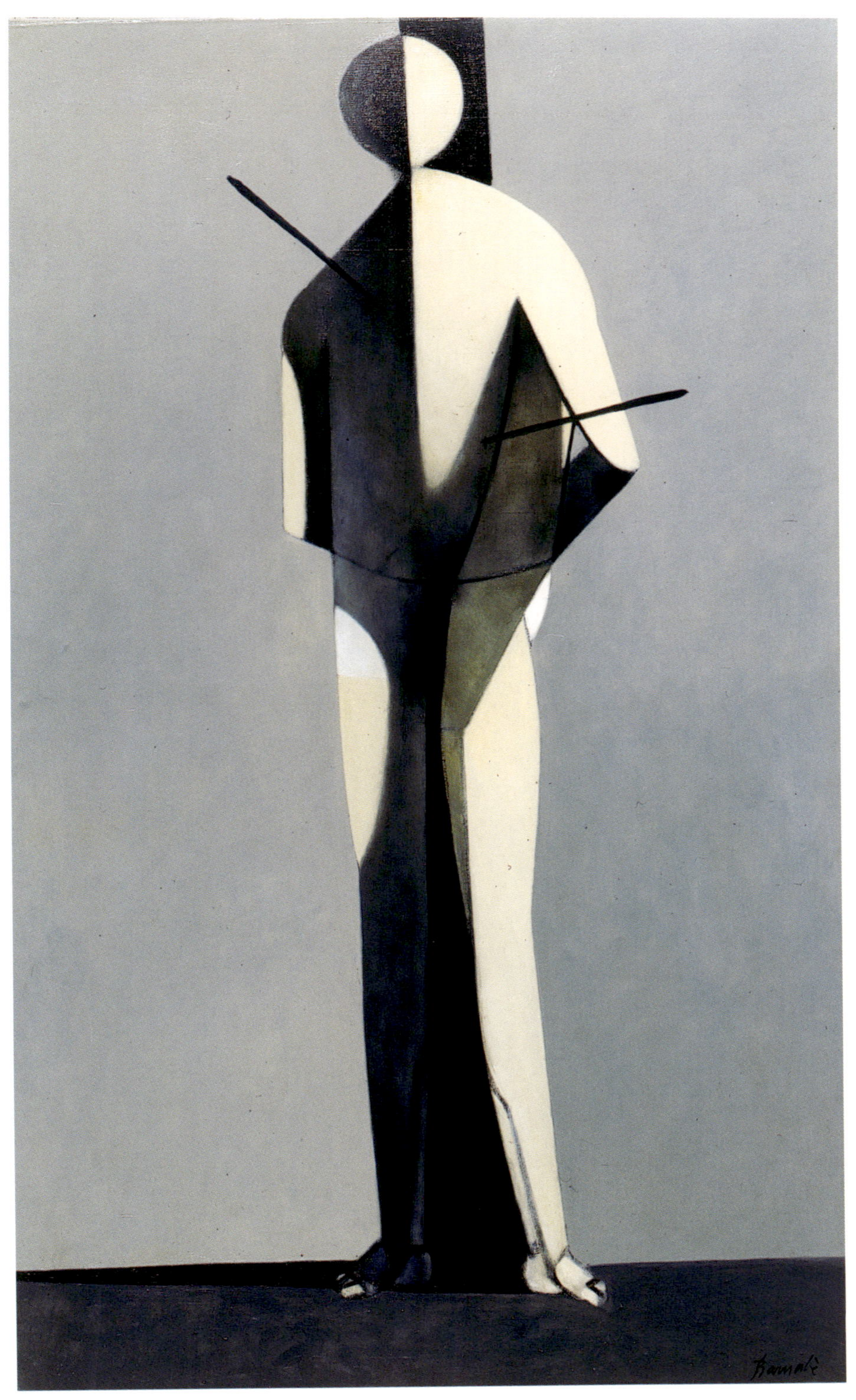

43. ***Pierrot in piedi***, about 1955
Pierrot Standing

Oil on canvas
145 x 96.5 cm.; 57 1/2 x 38 in.
Signed, lower right

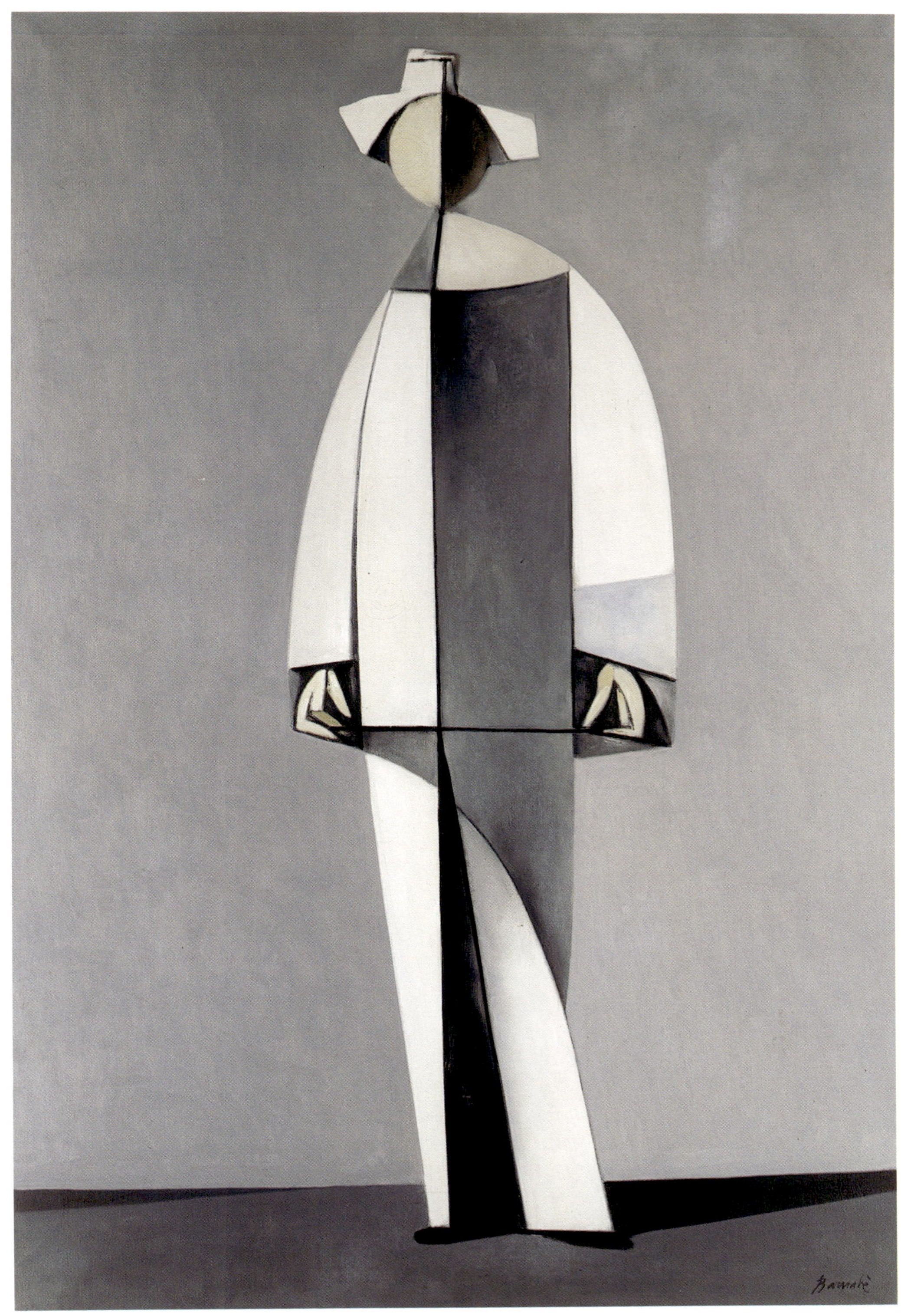

44. ***Suora di San Vincenzo,*** about 1955
Vincentian Nun

Oil on canvas
146 x 115 cm.; 57 1/2 x 46 1/2 inches
Signed, lower right

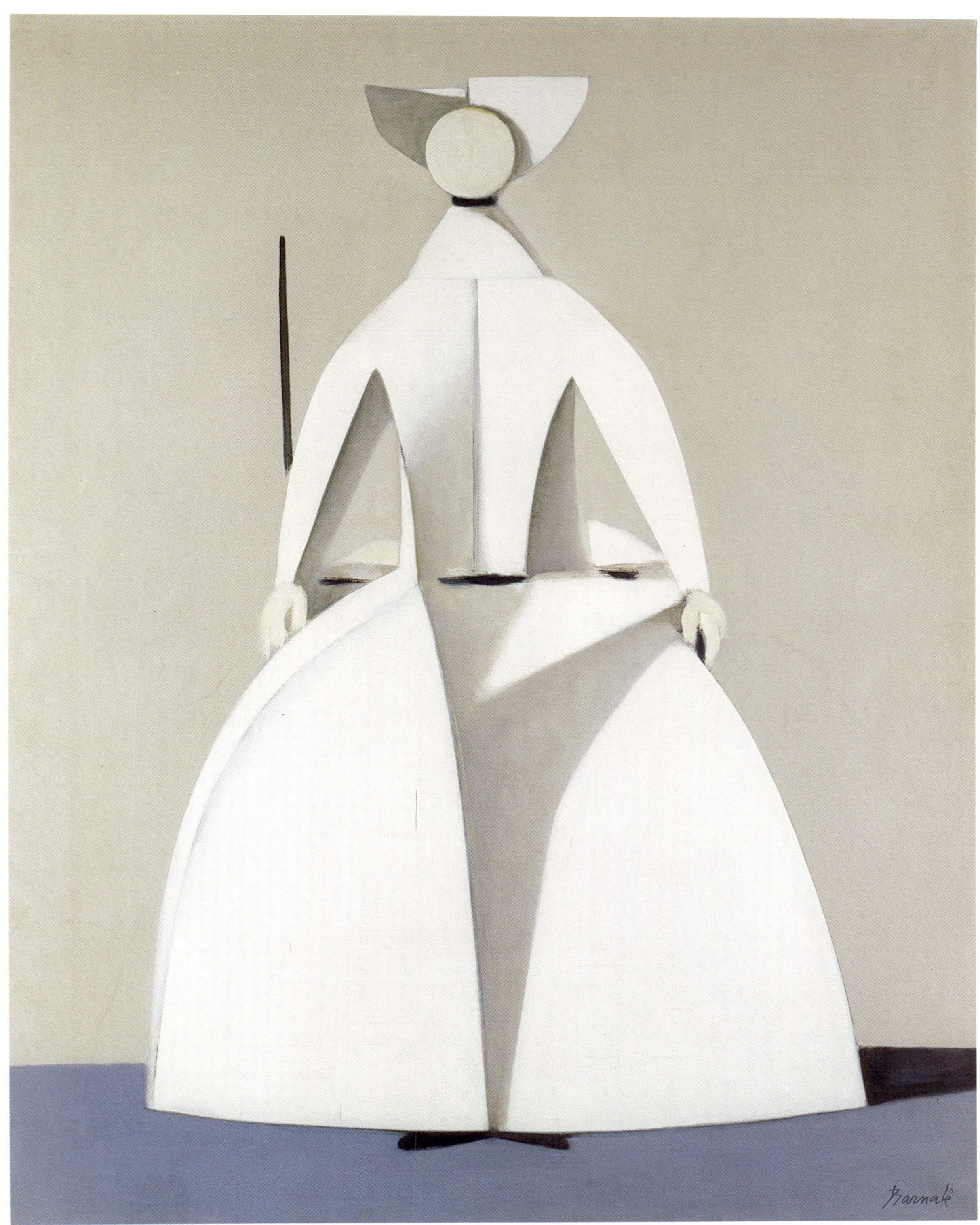

45. ***Figure seduta, fondo giallo***, about 1956
   Figure sitting: yellow background

   Oil on canvas
   100 x 81 cm.; 39 1/4 x 32 inches
   Signed, lower right

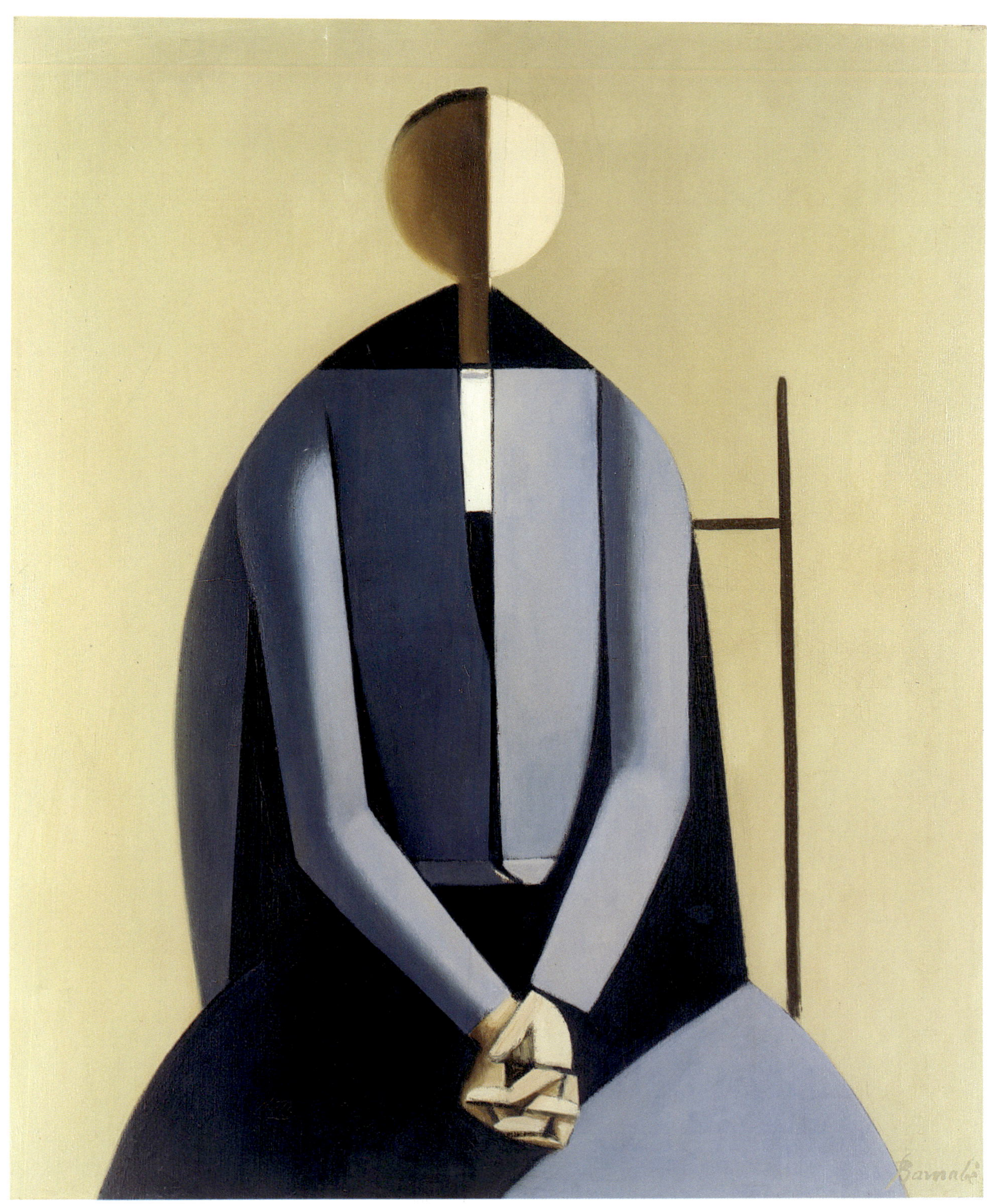

46. ***Due suore,*** about 1956
Two Nuns

Oil on canvas
81 x 100 cm.; 32 x 39 1/2 inches
Signed, lower right

Collection:
A private collection, Boca Raton

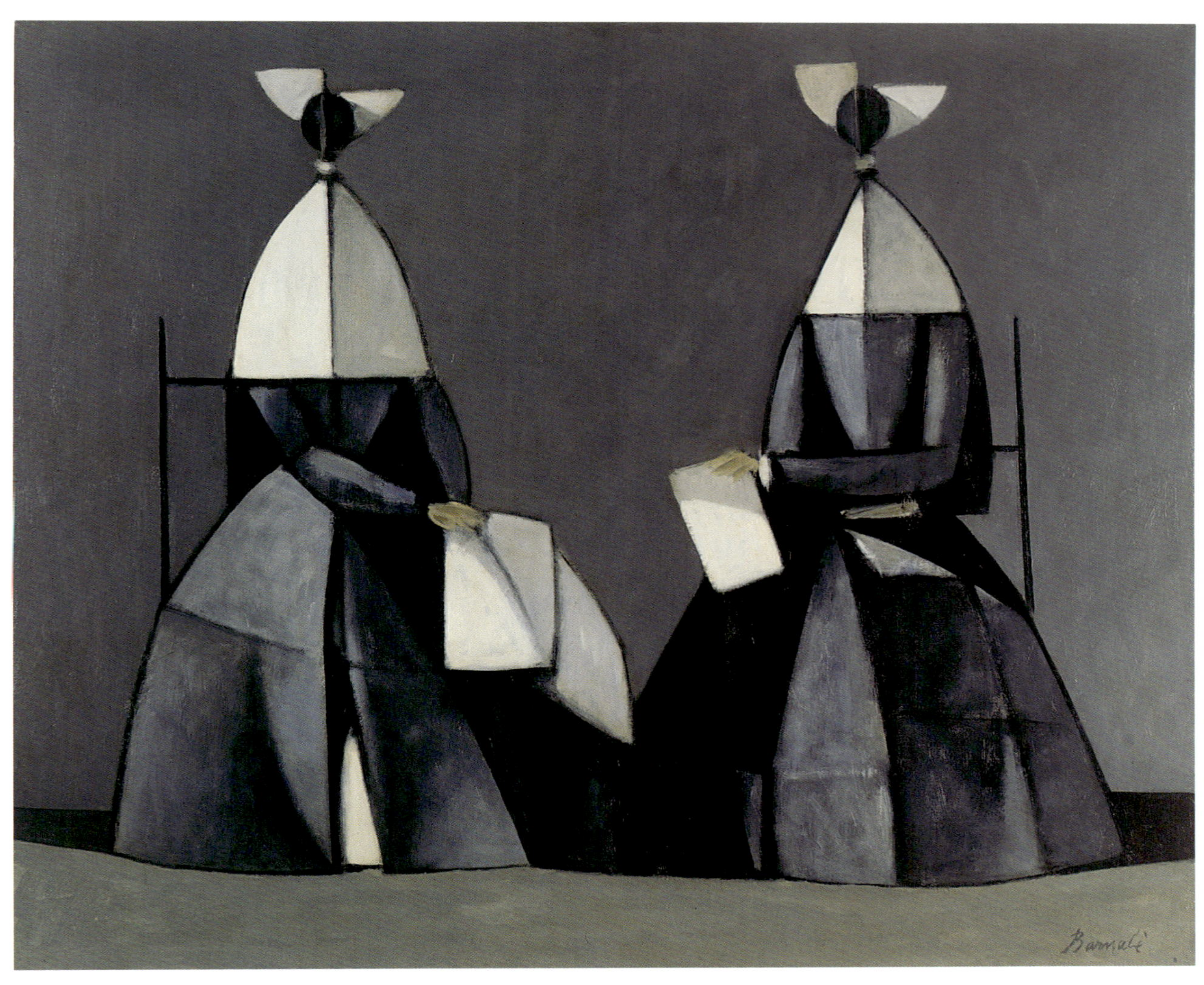

47. ***Donna in verde seduta,*** about 1956-57
Woman in Green, Seated

Oil on canvas
116.2 x 89.2 cm.; 45 3/4 x 35 1/8 inches
Signed, lower right

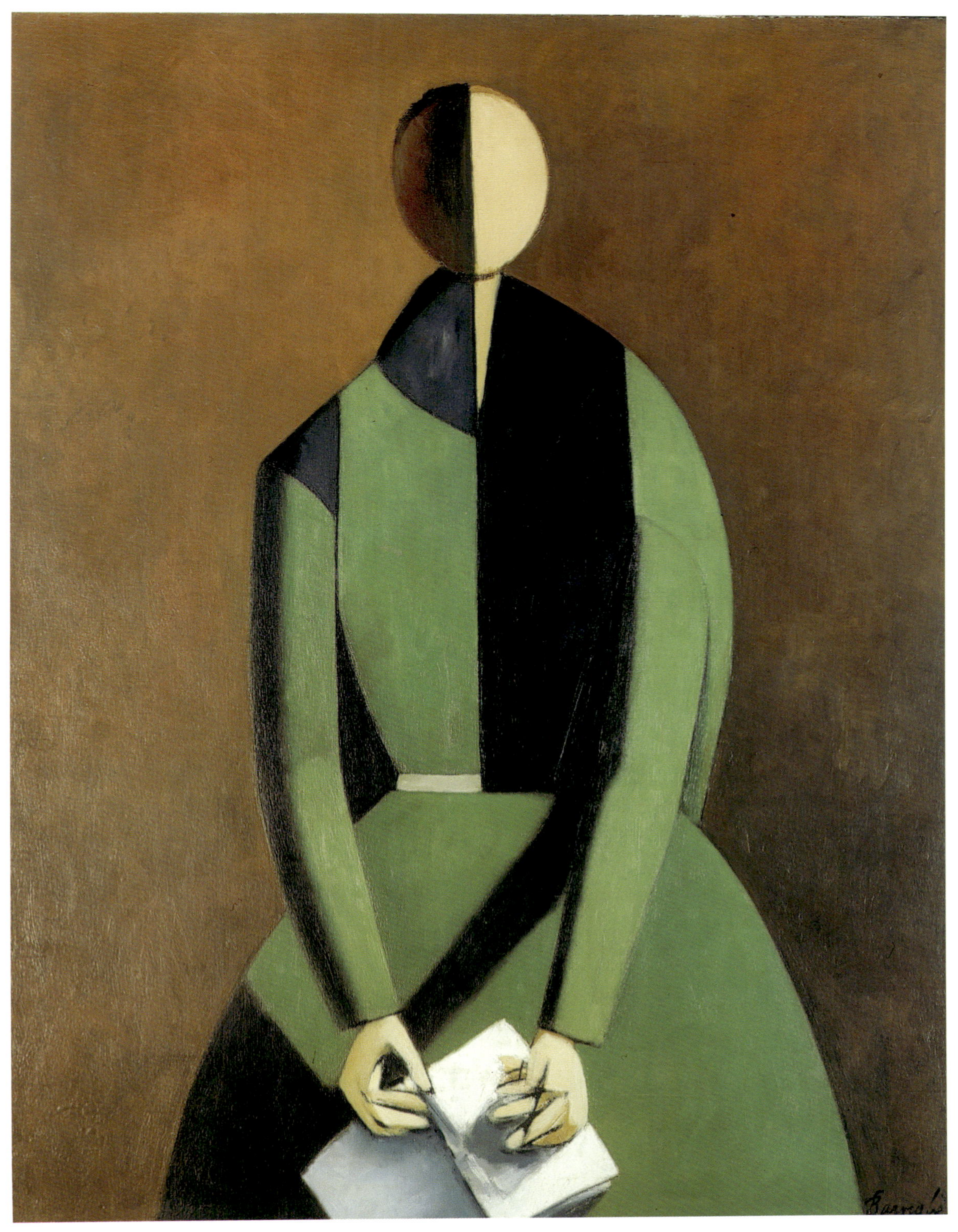

48. ***Natura morta con pere,*** about 1957
   Still Life with Pears

   Oil on canvas
   60 x 81 cm.; 23 3/4 x 32 inches
   Signed, lower right

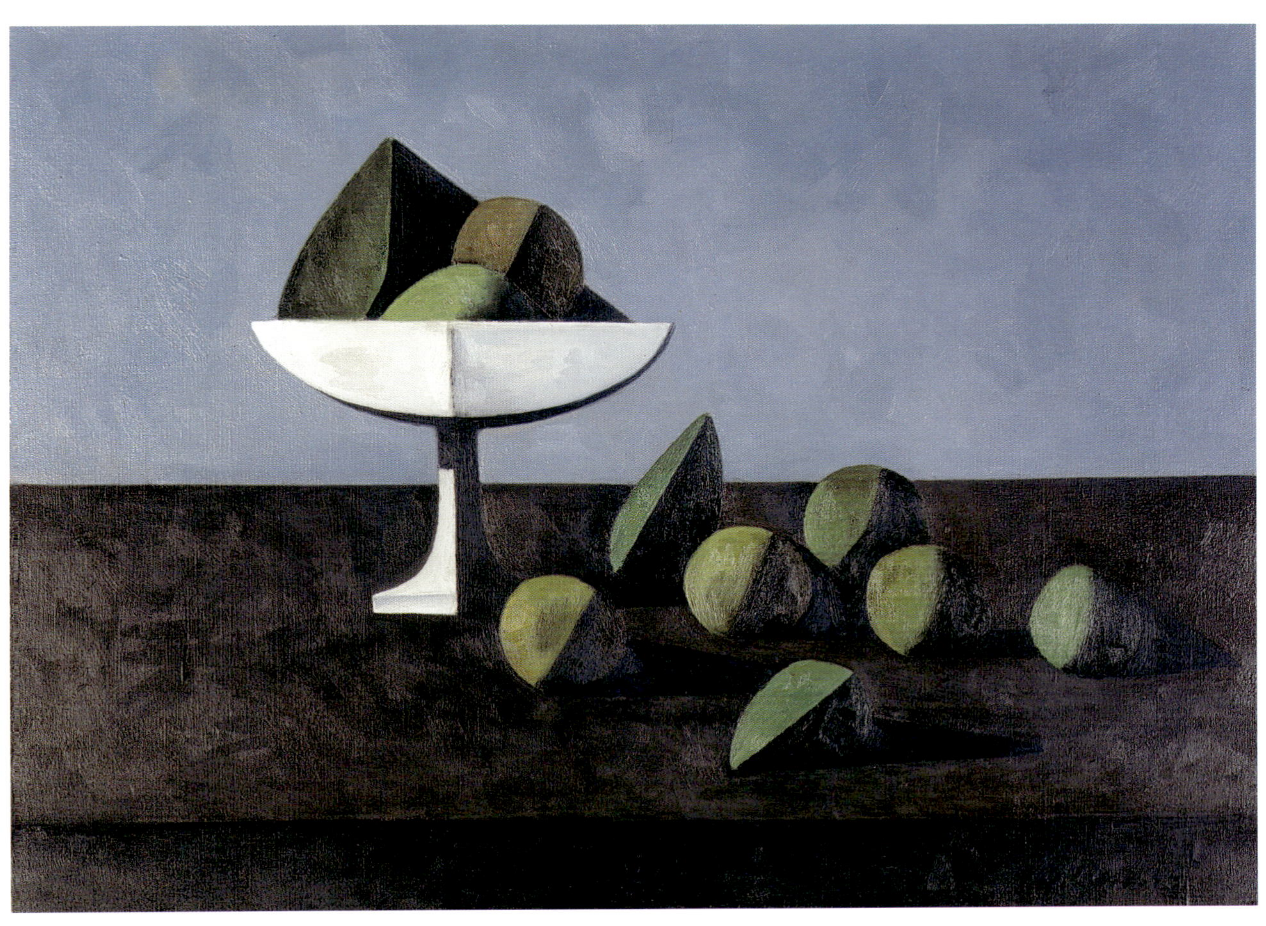

49. *Natura morta,* about 1957-58
Still Life

Oil on canvas
33 x 53 cm.; 13 1/8 x 21 3/4 inches
Signed, lower right

Formerly collection:
Mr. and Mrs. Kirk Douglas

Collection:
Dale and Betsey Pinkert

50. *Mazzo di fiori,* about 1956-57

Oil on canvas
24.4 x 19.4 cm.; 9 1/2 x 7 1/2 inches
Signed, lower right

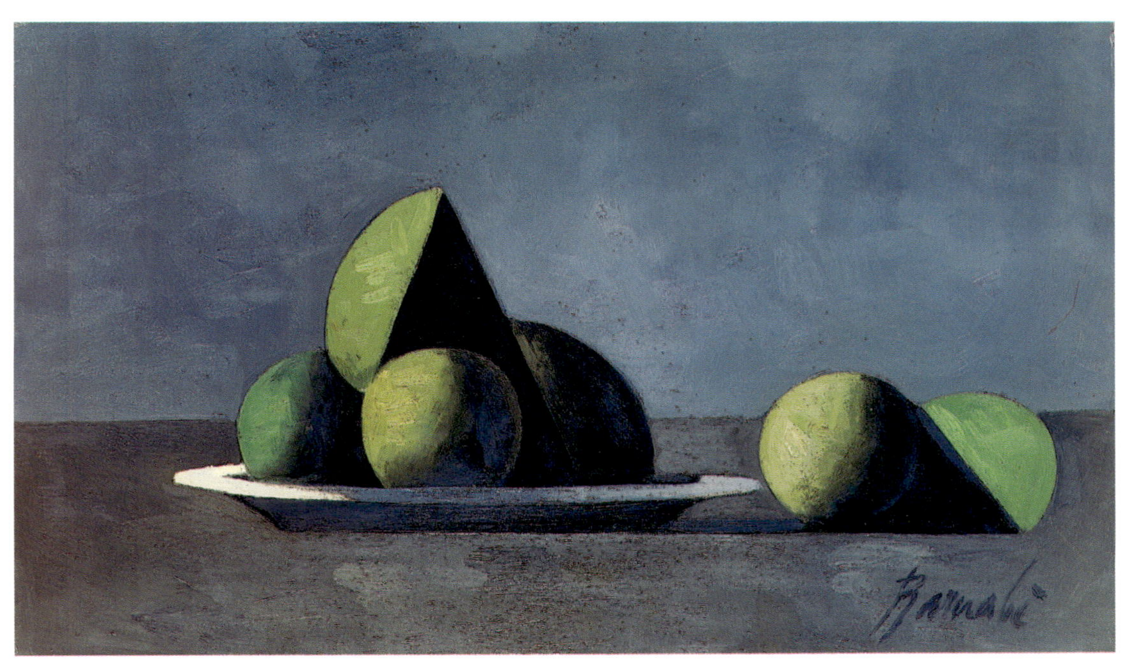

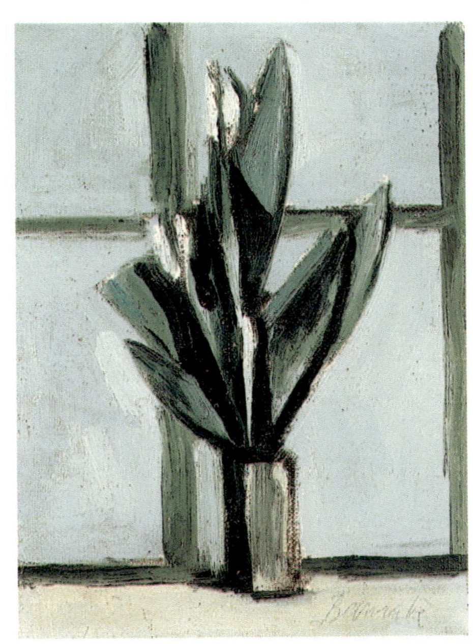

51. ***Figura, ad un tavolo con natura morta,*** about 1957
Figure at a Table with Still Life

Oil on canvas
114 x 145 cm.; 45 x 57 1/4 inches
Signed, lower right

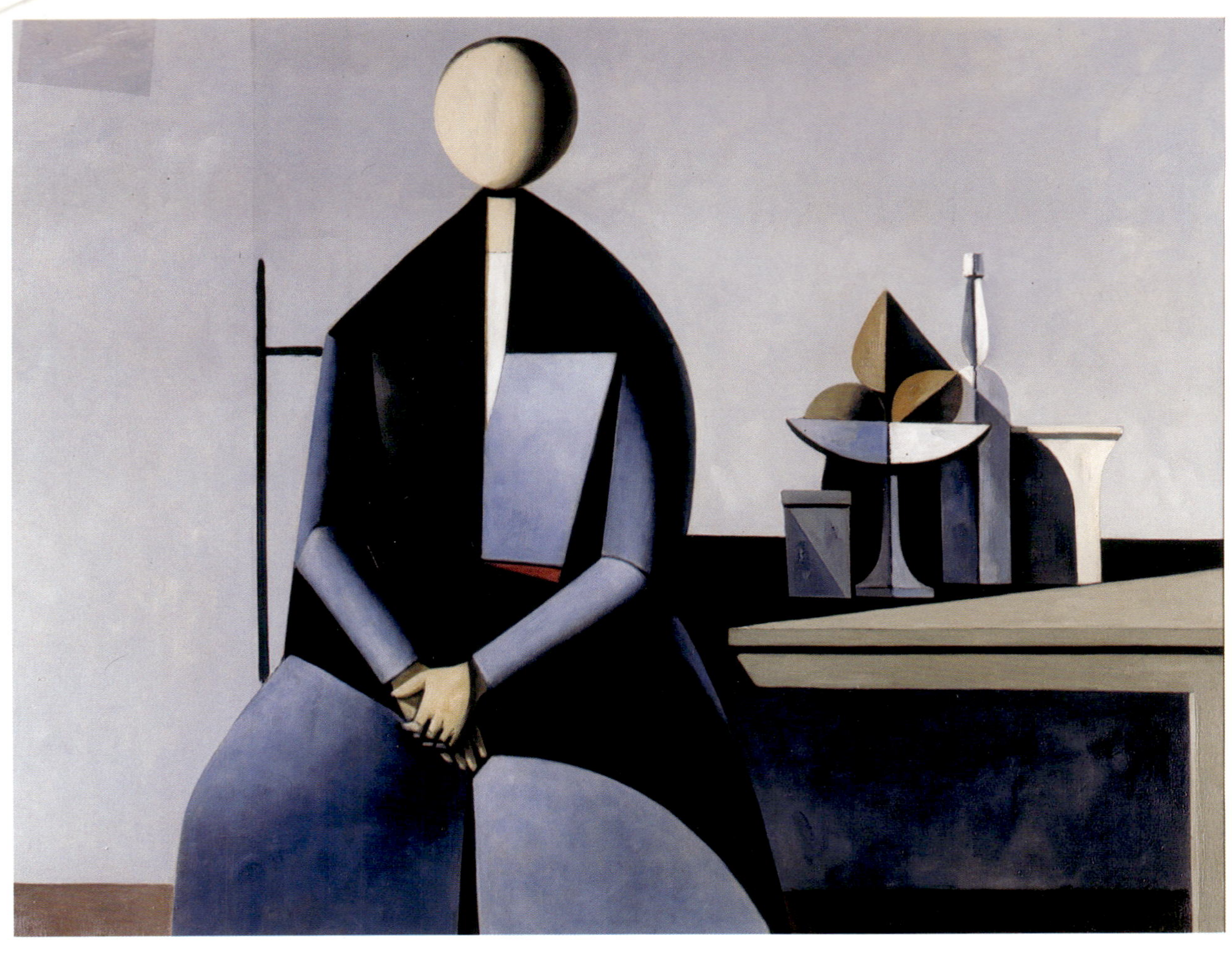

52. ***Due figure sedute al tavolo***, about 1958
Two Figures at a Table

Oil on canvas
24 x 35 cm.; 9 3/8 x 13 3/4 inches
Signed, lower right

53. **Pierrot,** about 1958
Pierrot

Oil on canvas
35 x 24 cm.; 13 3/4 x 9 3/8 inches
Signed in pencil, lower right

54. ***Uomo seduto***, 1958
Man Seated

Oil on canvas
35.3 x 24.4 cm.; 13 3/4 x 9 1/2 inches
Signed and dated on verso "Barnabé 1958"

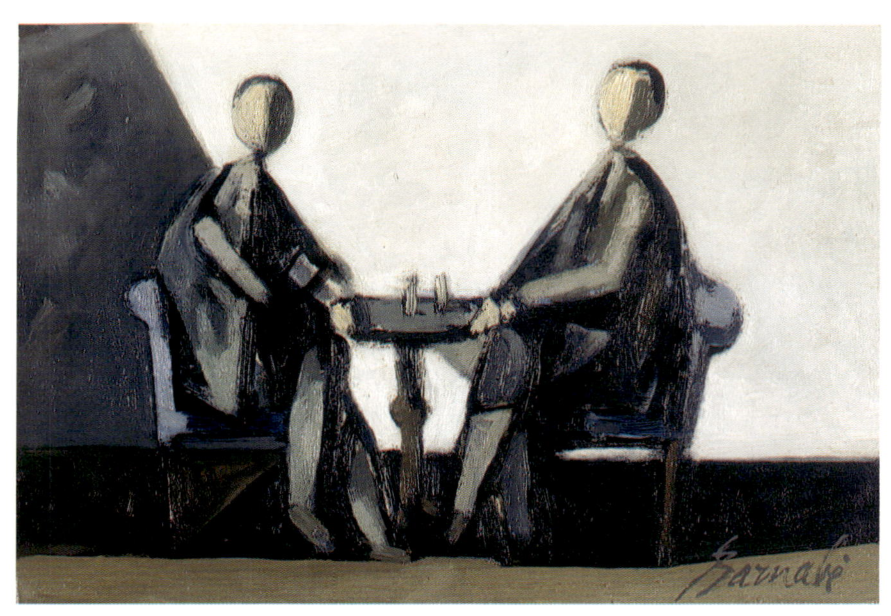

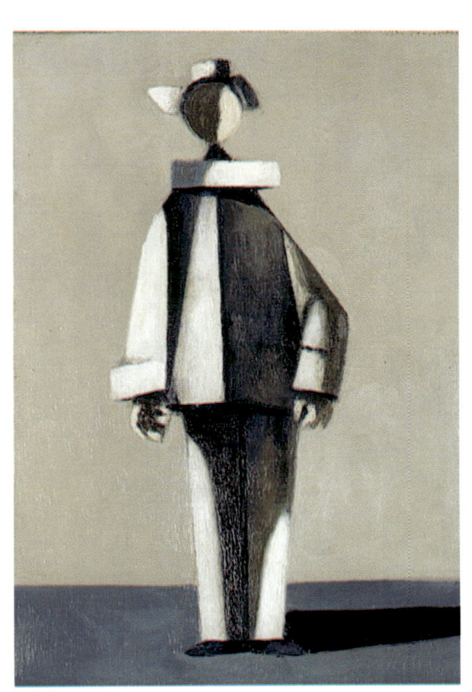

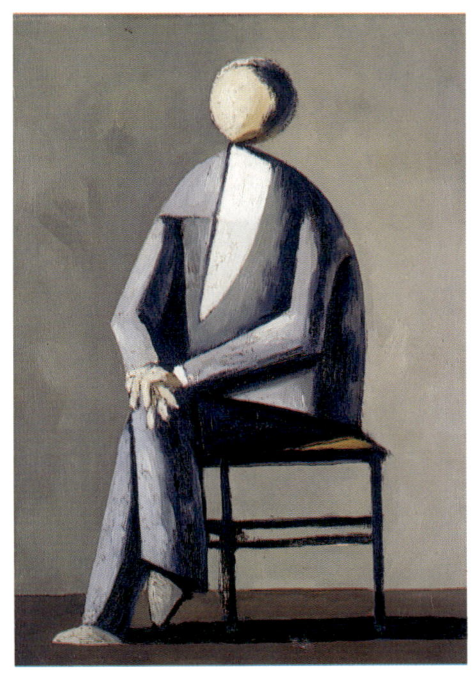

55. ***Natura morta,*** April 28, 1958
Still Life

Oil on canvas
85 x 70 cm.; 33 1/2 x 27 1/2 inches
Signed, lower right

Verso:
Signed and dated

Collection:
Mr. and Mrs. Jim Mack

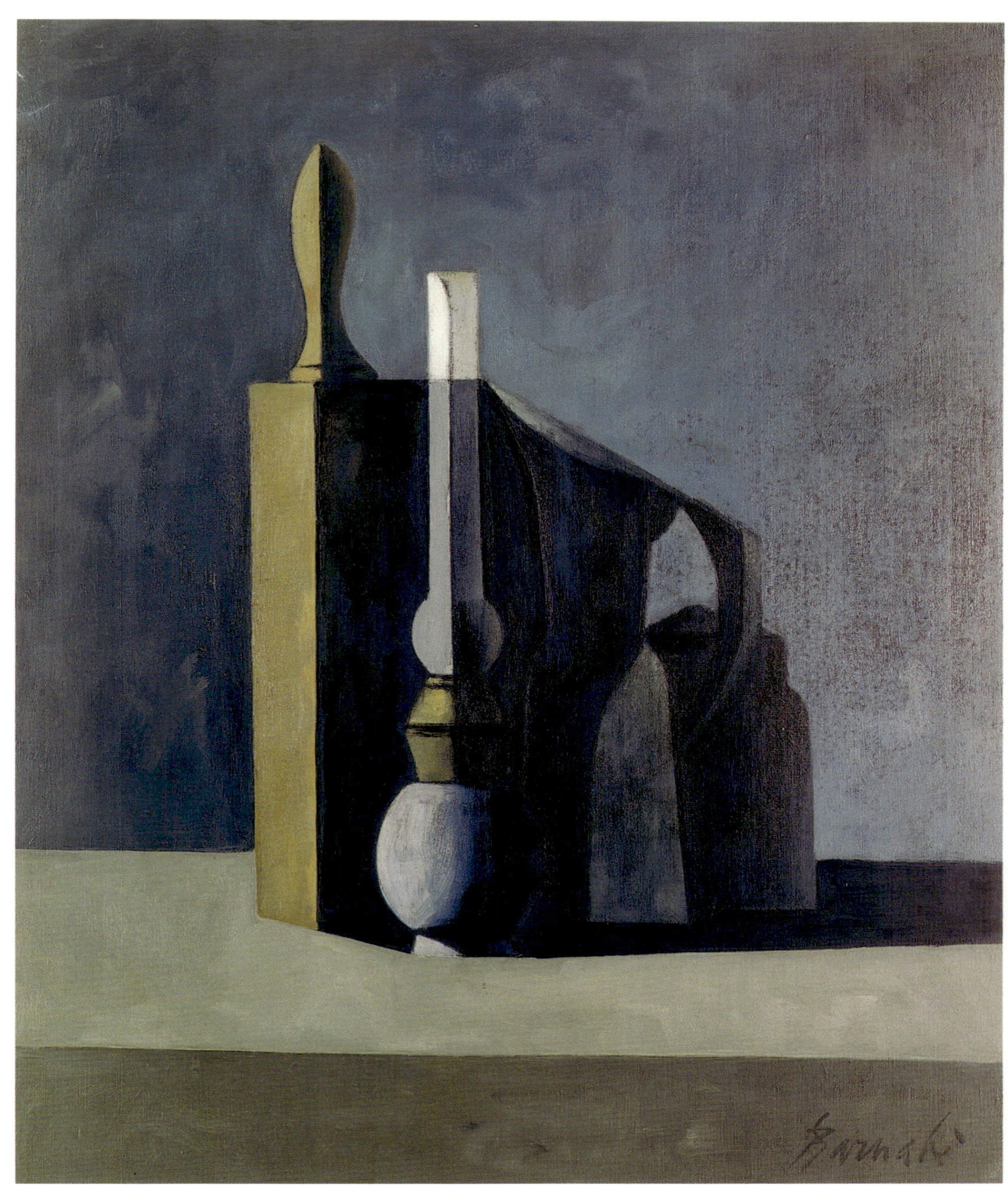

56. *Natura morta,* about 1958
    Still Life

    Oil on canvas
    50 x 100 cm.; 19 5/8 x 39 1/4 inches
    Signed, lower right

    Collection:
    Private Collection

57. *Natura morta,* 1958
    Still Life

    Oil on canvas
    50.2 x 100 cm.; 19 3/4 x 39 1/4 inches
    Signed, lower right

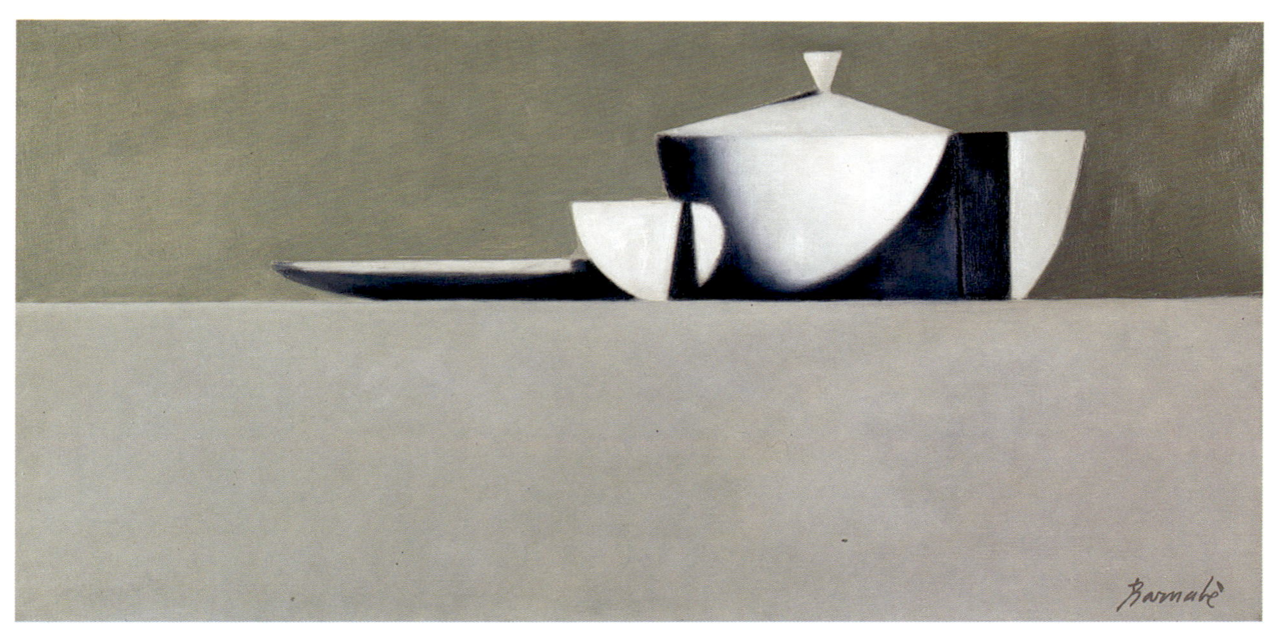

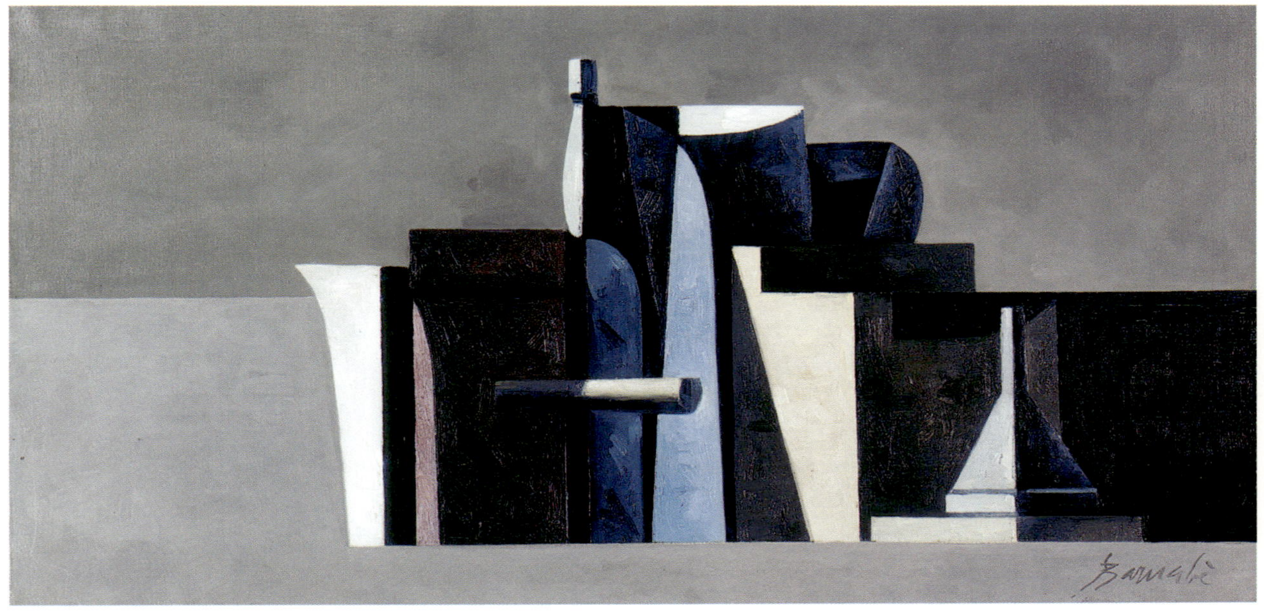

58. *Natura morta,* 1958
   Still Life

   Oil on canvas
   65 x 92 cm.; 25 1/2 x 36 1/4 inches
   Signed, lower right

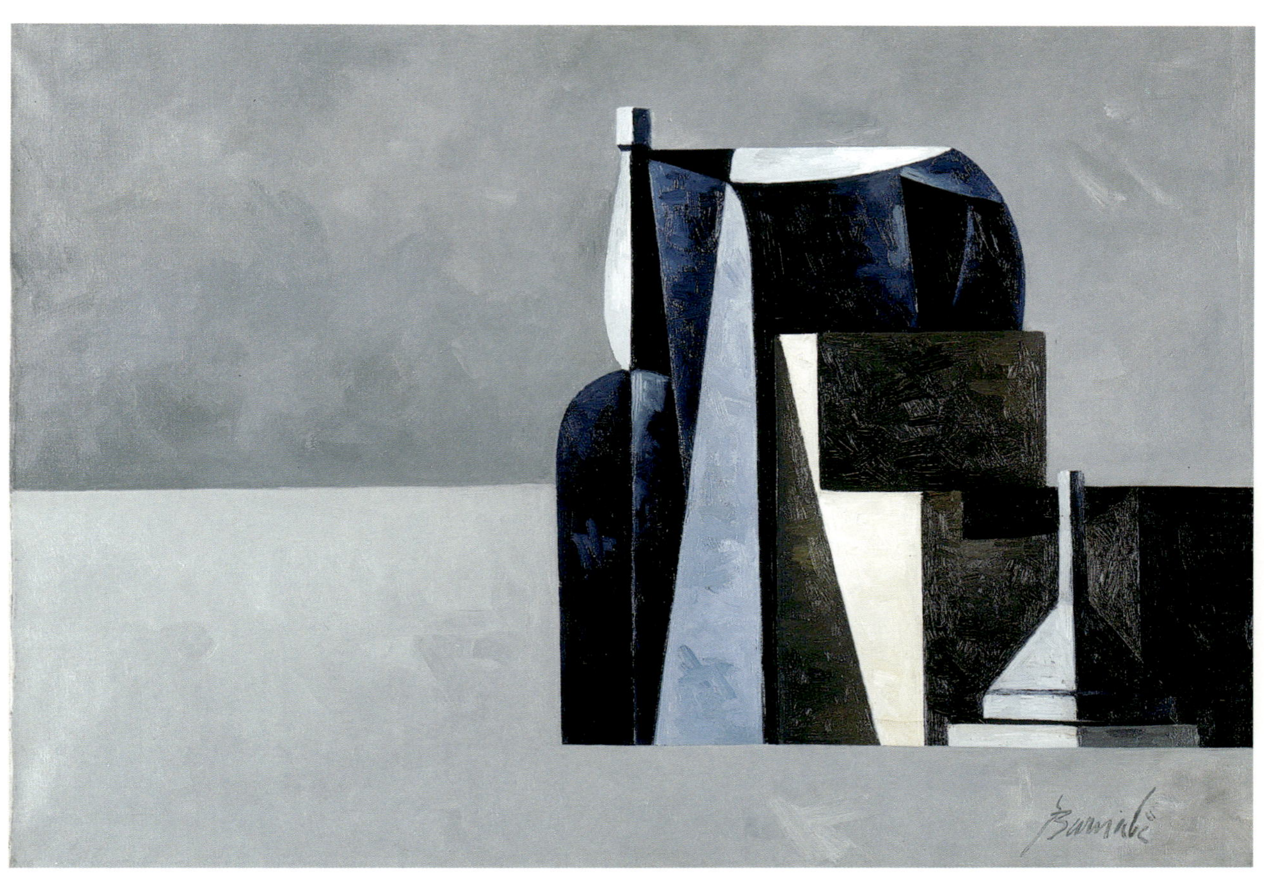

59. ***Natura morta su fondo blu***, 1958
Still Life with Blue Background

Oil on canvas
81 x 100 cm.; 32 x 39 1/2 inches
Signed, lower right

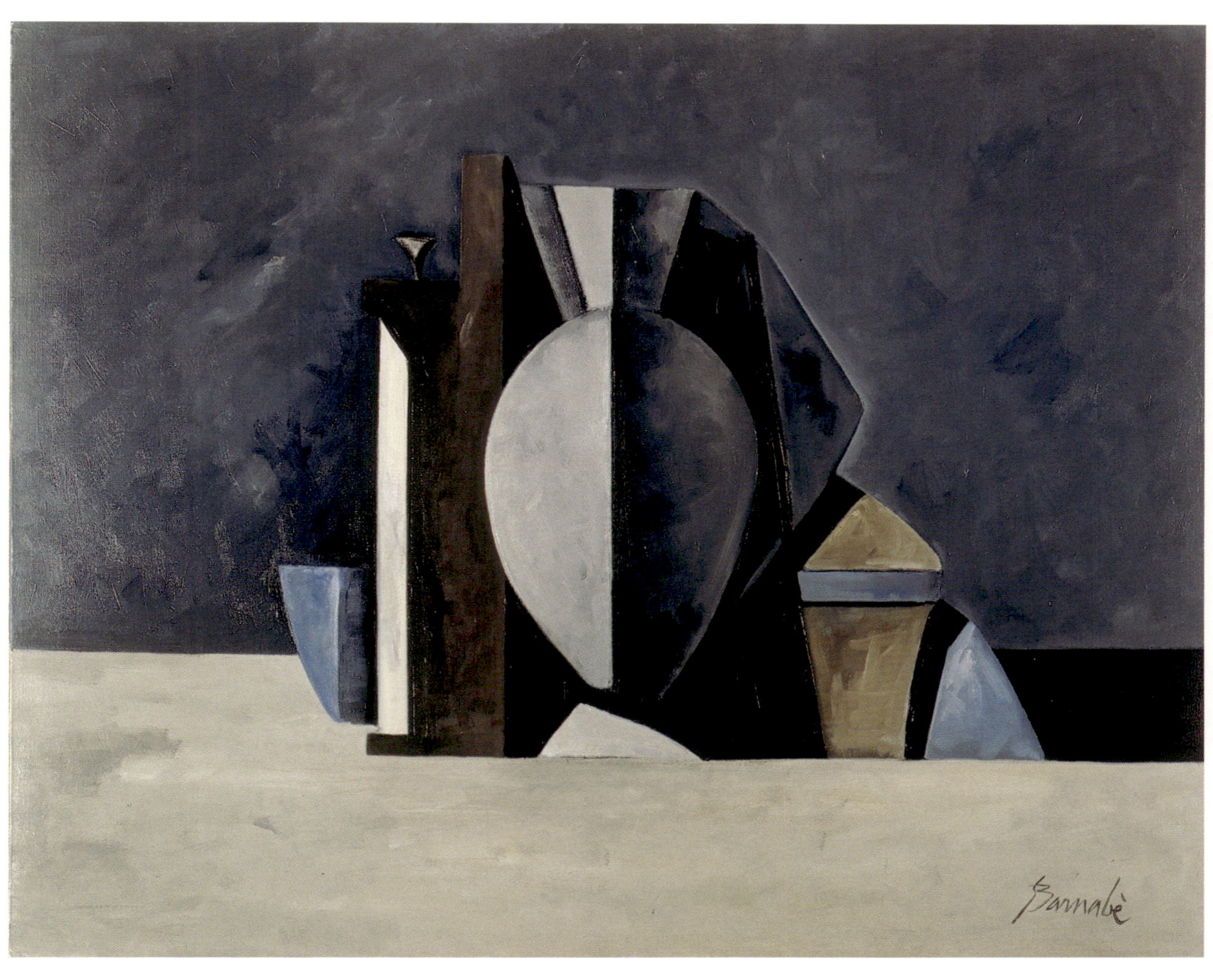

60. ***Natura morta***, about 1958
   Still Life

   Oil on canvas
   73 x 91 cm.; 28 3/4 x 36 1/4 inches
   Signed, lower right

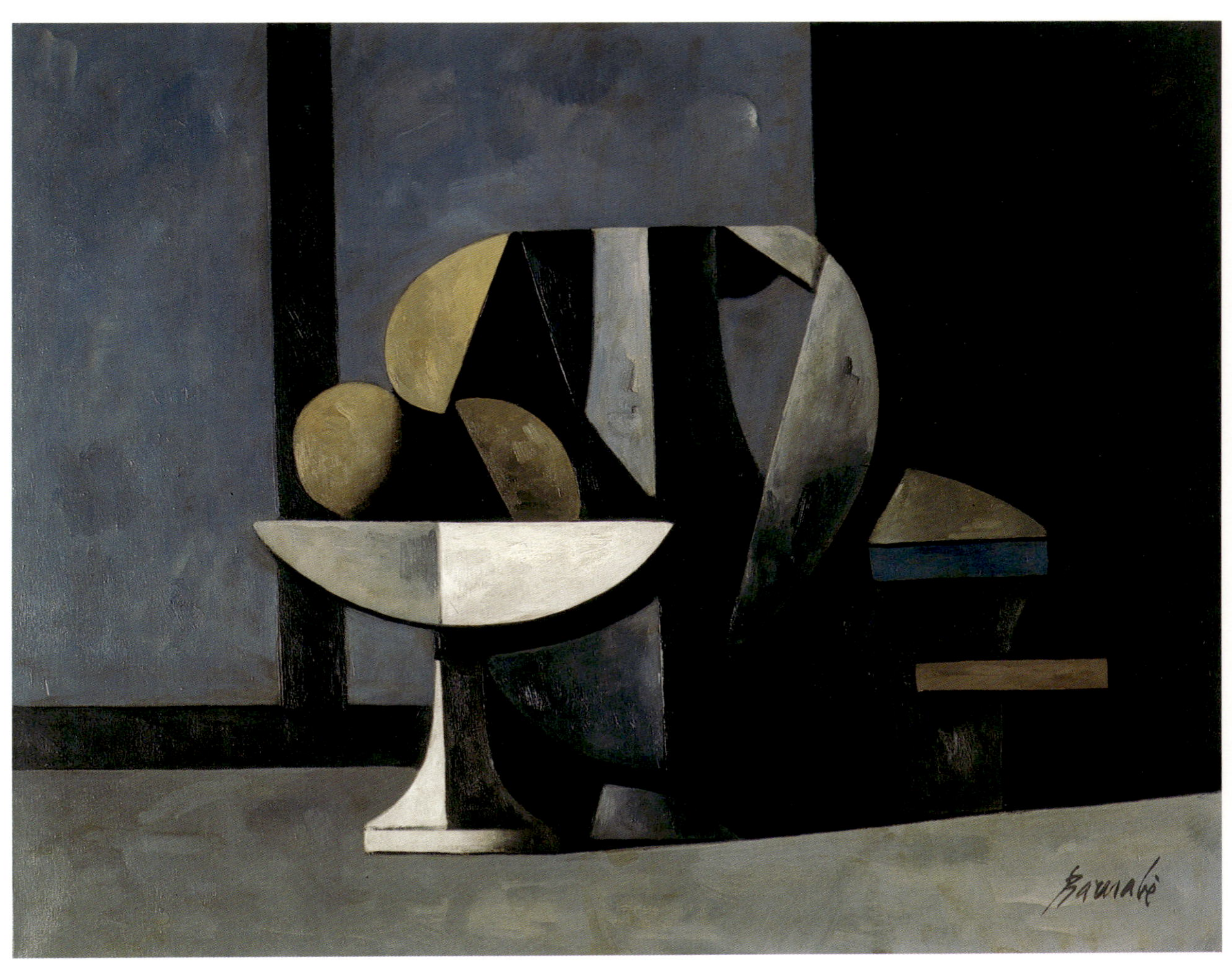

Barnabé

61. *__Mazzo di fiori,__* about 1958
Bouquet

Oil on canvas
100 x 100 cm.; 39 1/4 x 39 1/4 inches
Signed, lower right

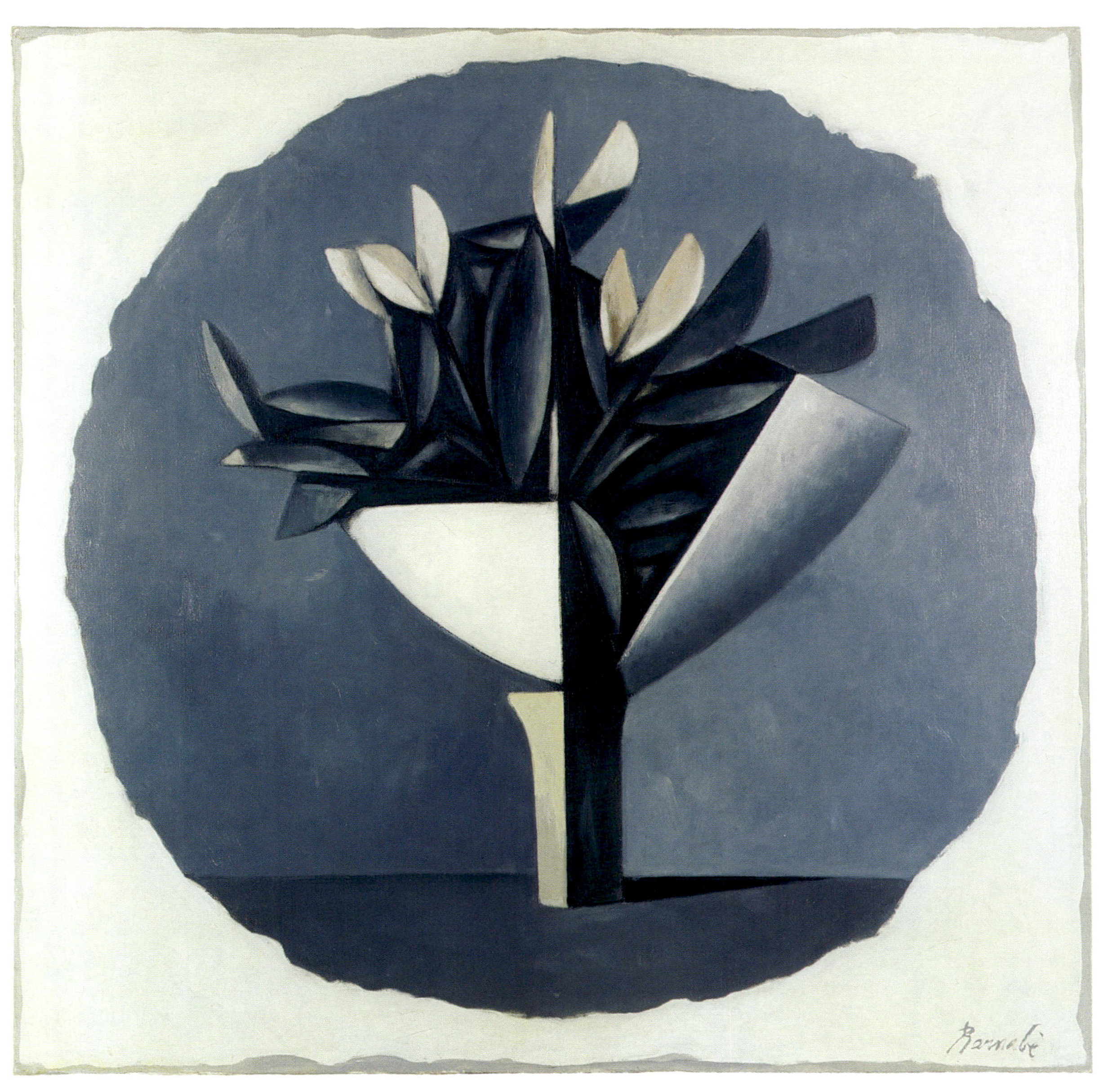
Barnabé

62. *Mazzo di fiori rosa e bianco,* about 1958
Bouquet in Pink and White

Oil on canvas
81.3 x 54 cm.; 32 x 21 1/4 inches
Signed, lower right

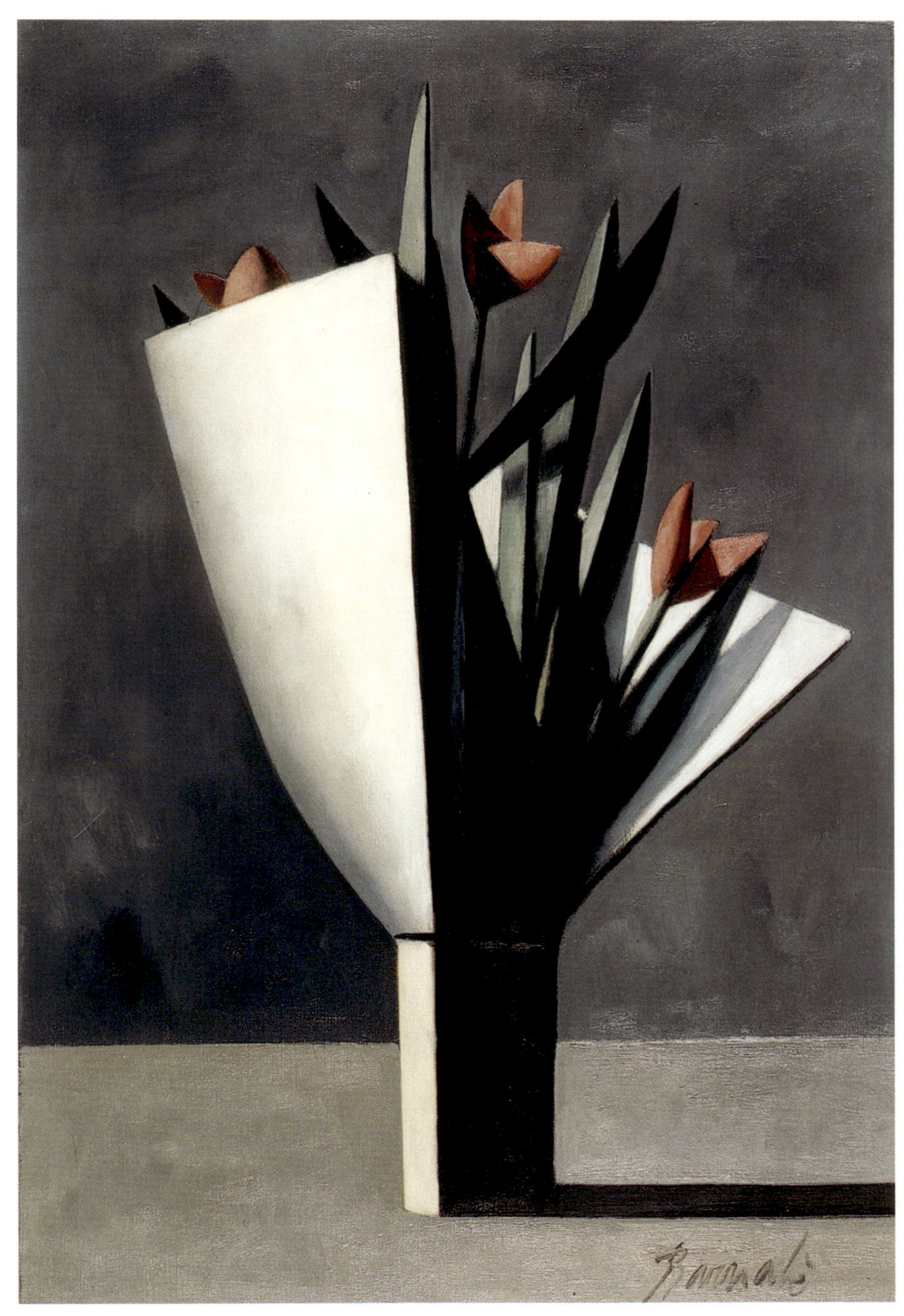

63. ***Mazzo di fiori con striscia blu,*** about 1958
Bouquet with Blue Stripe

Oil on canvas
50.5 x 64.8 cm.; 19 7/8 x 25 1/2 inches
Signed, lower right

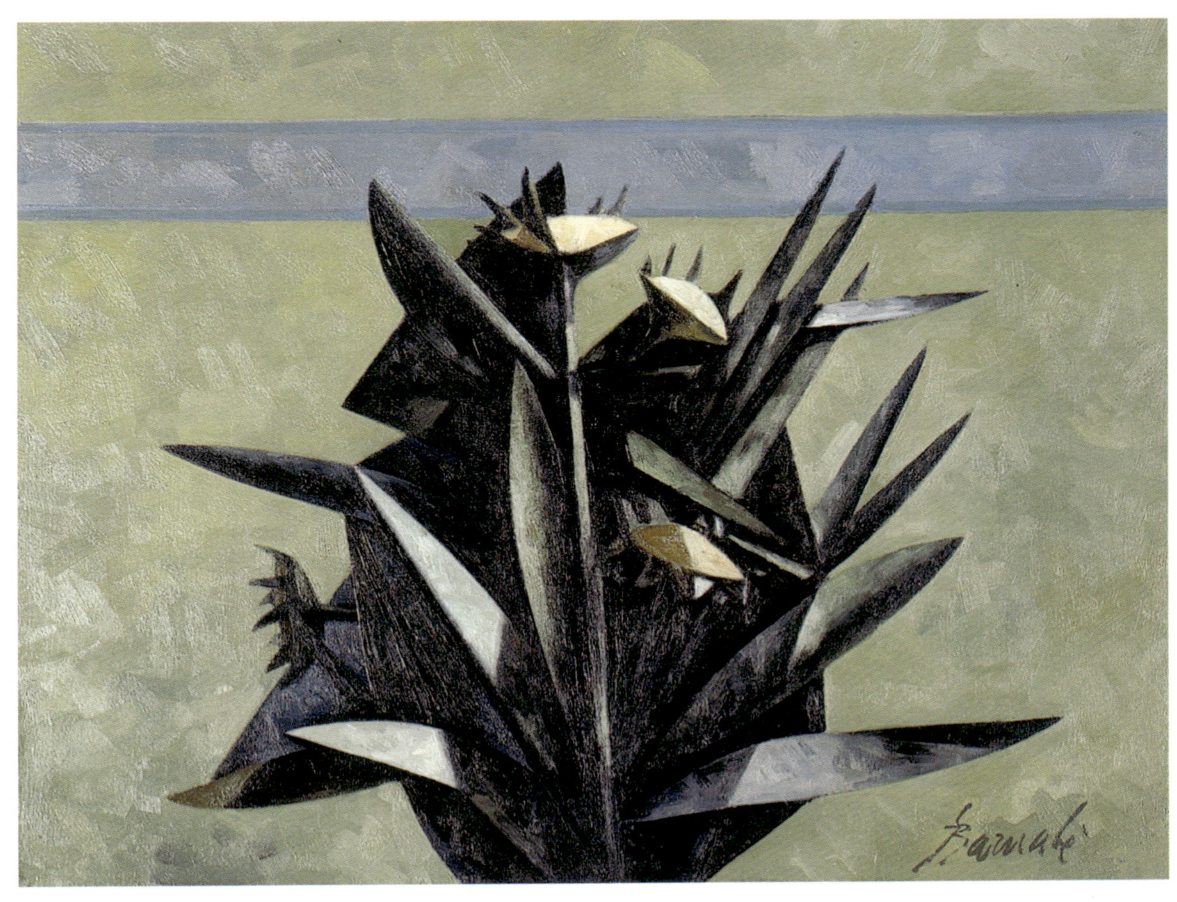

64. *Mazzo di fiori,* 1958
Bouquet

Charcoal drawing
62.2 x 48.2 cm.; 24 1/2 x 19 inches
Signed with brush lower right
Signed and dated in charcoal on verso: "26 febbraio 1958 Barnabè"
Dedicated in charcoal on verso: "A Monsieur James Wise avec sympathie. Barnabè 10 mai 1958"

Notes:
James Wise was an American scholar and dealer who lived near Avignon, in southern France.

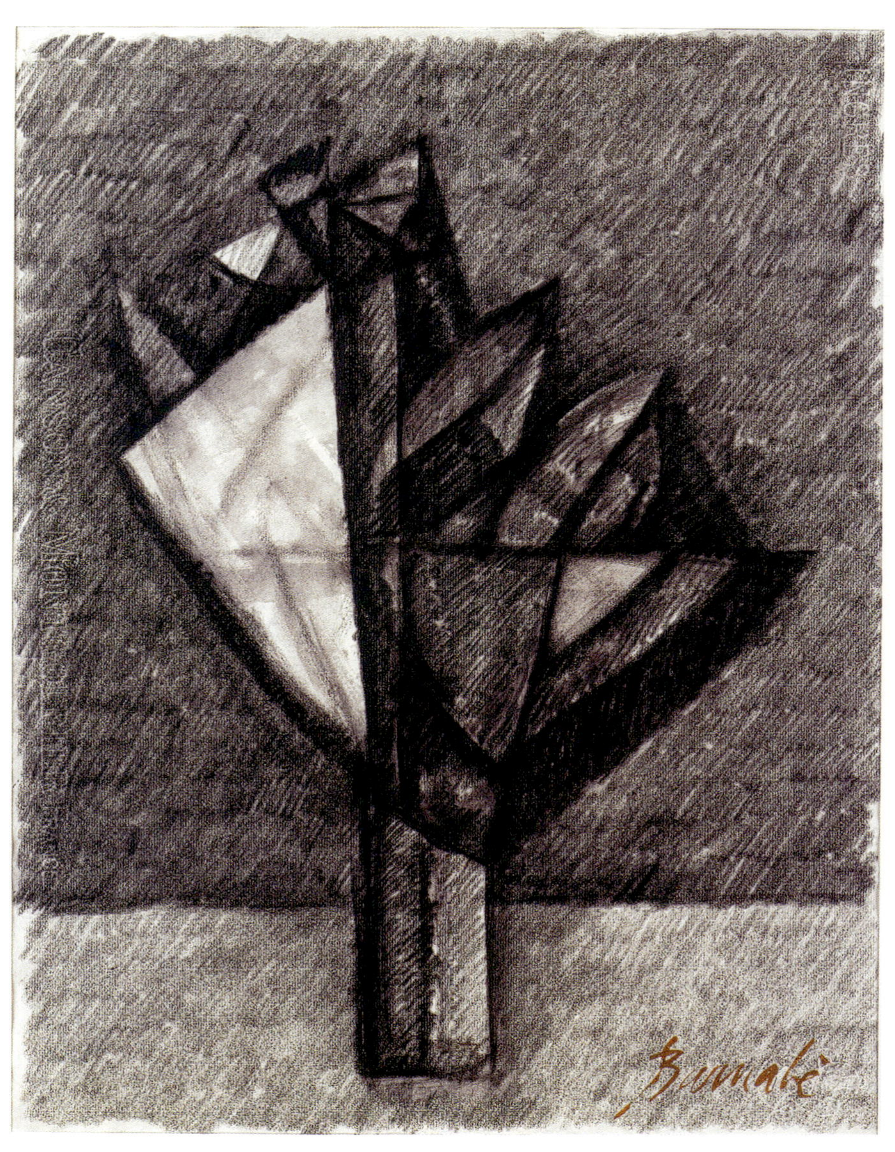

65. ***Arlecchino in blu e grigio***, about 1958
Harlequin in Blue and Gray

Charcoal and gouache
65.5 x 50.5 cm.; 25 3/4 x 19 7/8 inches
Signed, lower right

66. ***Ragazza con libro***, about 1958
Girl with Book

Gouache and pastel
65.5 x 50.5 cm.; 25 3/4 x 19 7/8 inches
Signed, lower right

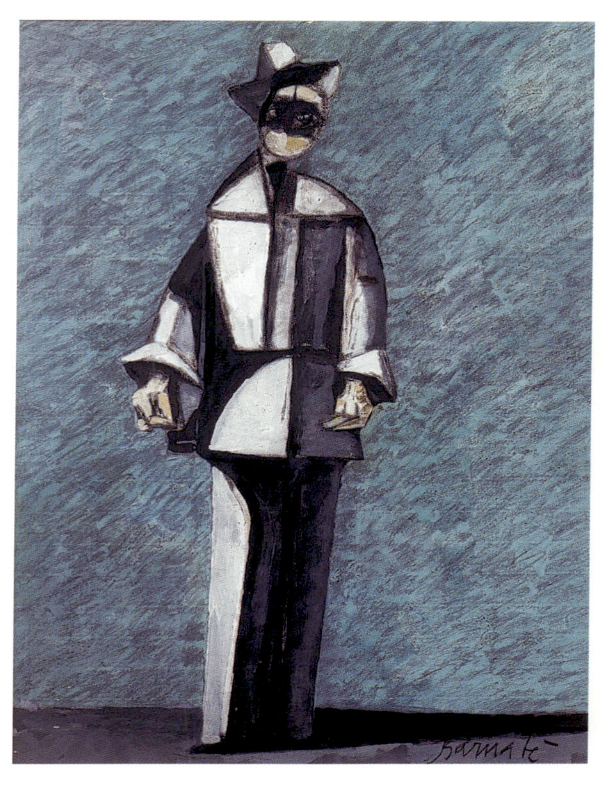

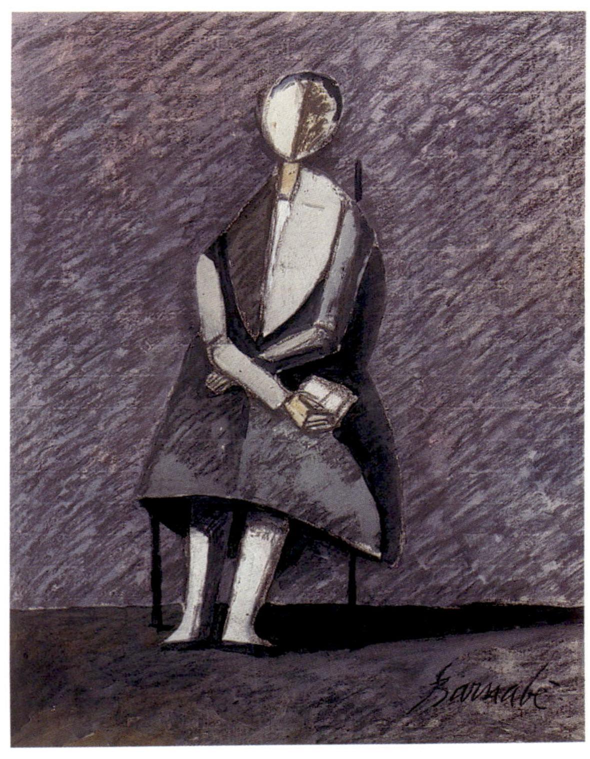

67. ***Paesaggio,*** 1959
Landscape

Oil on canvas
65 x 92 cm.; 25 3/4 x 36 inches
Signed and dated, lower right

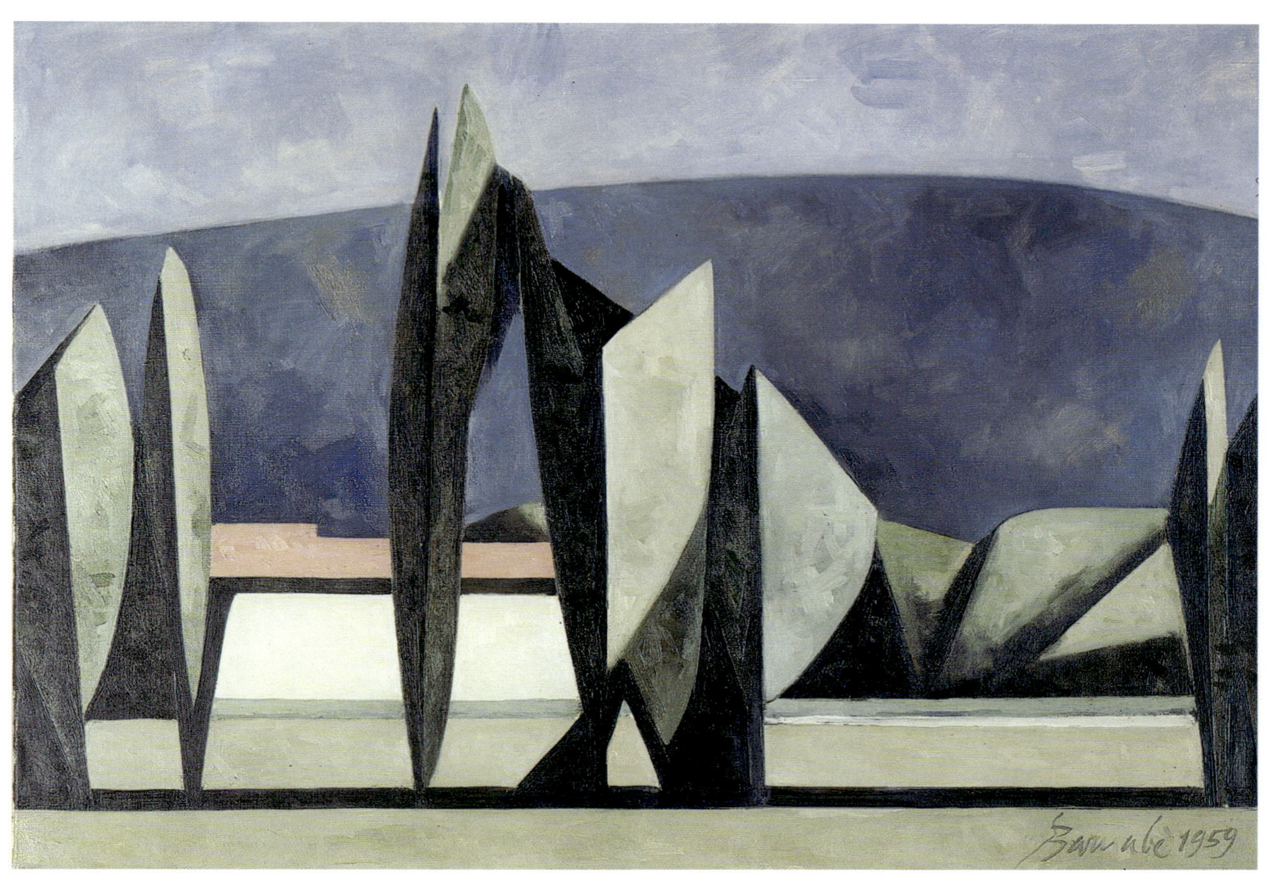

68. ***Merenda all'aperto***, about 1959
    Picnic

    Oil on canvas
    46 x 55 cm.; 18 1/8 x 21 5/8 inches
    Signed, lower right

69. ***Paesaggio con alberi,*** about 1959
    Landscape with Trees

    Oil on canvas
    32.5 x 45.5 cm.; 13 1/4 x 18 3/8
    Signed, lower right

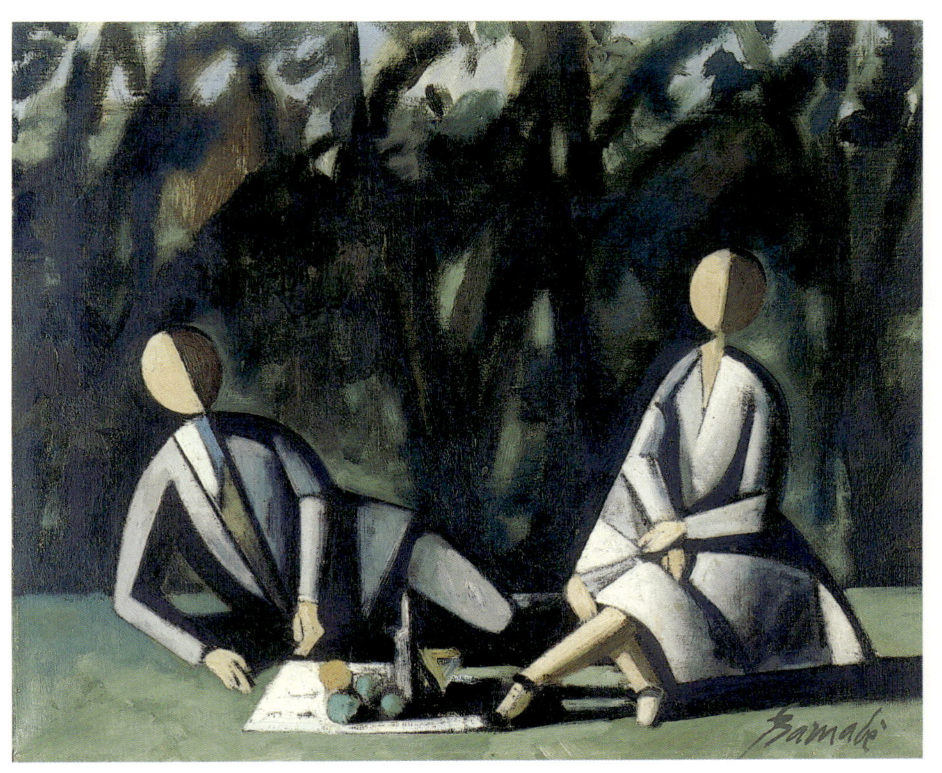

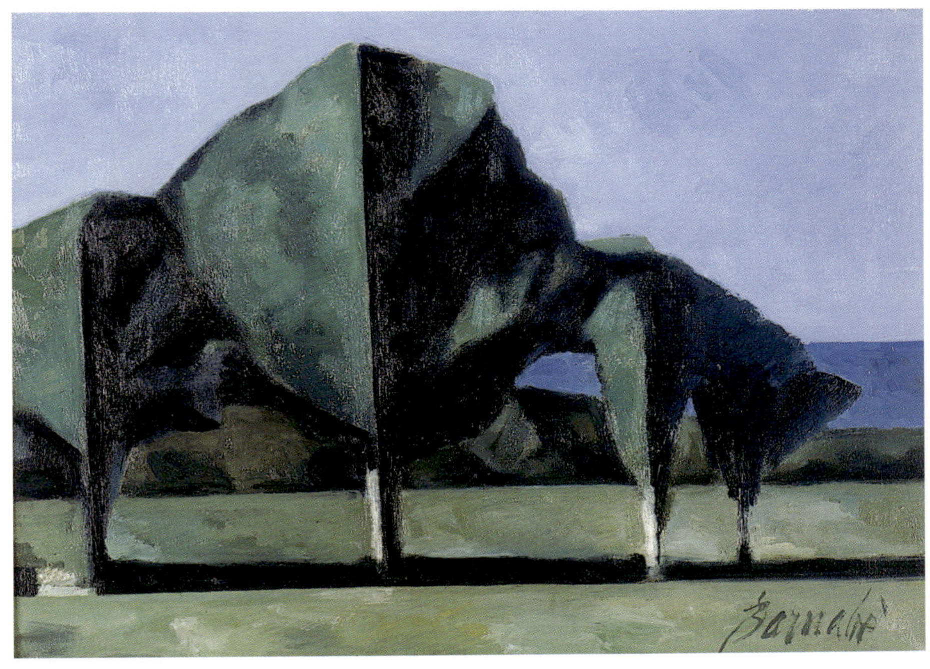

70. ***Pescatori***, about 1959
    Fishermen

    Oil on canvas
    46.4 x 55.2 cm.; 18 1/4 x 21 3/4 inches
    Signed, lower right

71. ***Uomo con capello***, about 1960
    Man with a Hat

    Oil on canvas
    35 x 27 cm.; 13 3/4 x 10 5/8 inches
    Signed, lower right

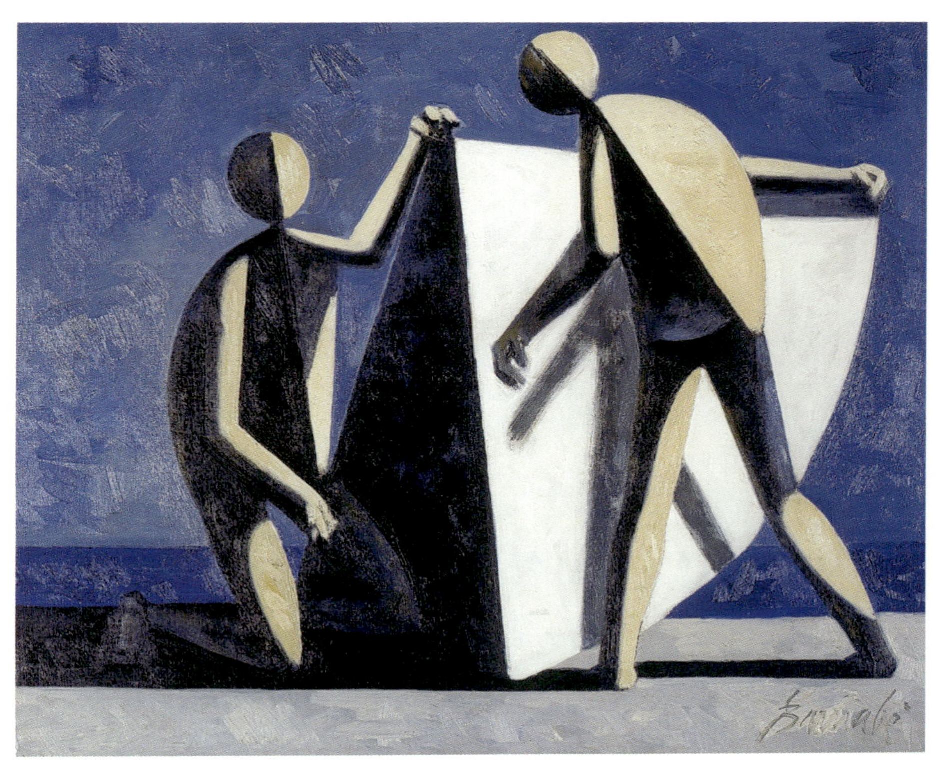

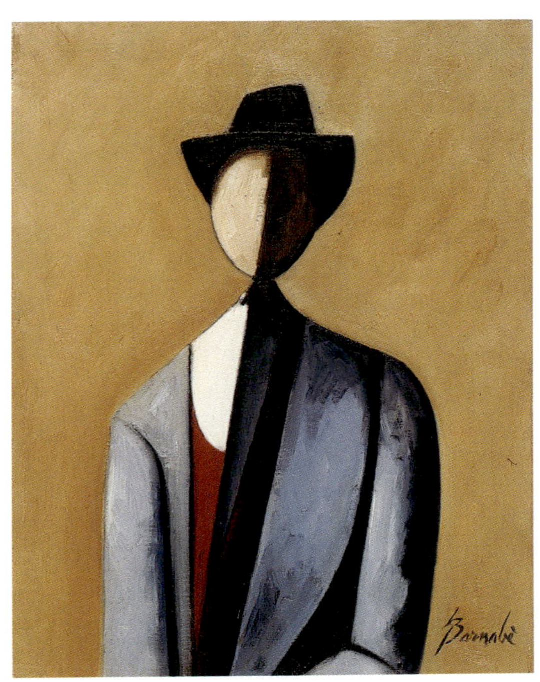

72. ***Mazzo di fiori su fondo rosa,*** 1959
   Bouquet with Rose Background

   Oil on canvas
   65.5 x 45 cm.; 25 3/4 x 17 3/4 inches
   Signed, lower left

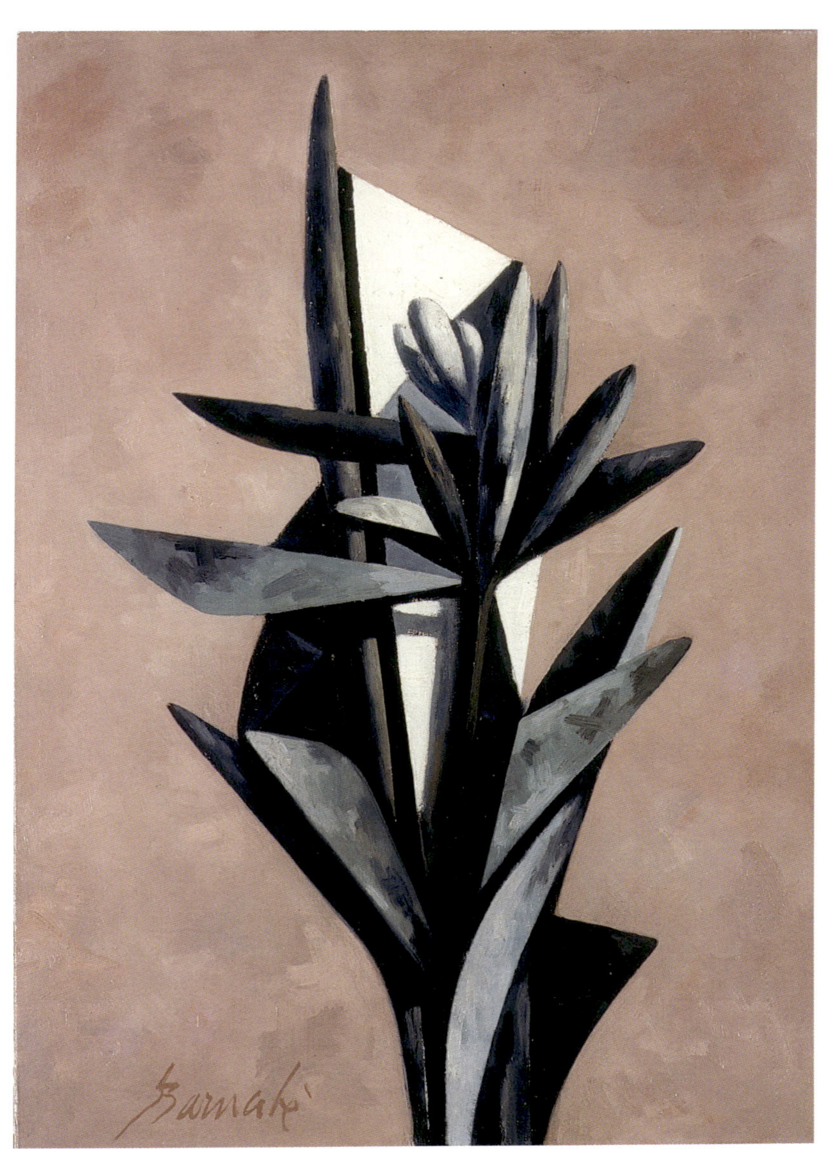

73. ***Mazzo di fiori sul tavolo grigio e blu***, 1959
Bouquet with Gray and Blue Table

Mixed media
63 x 48 cm.; 24 3/4 x 19 inches
Signed and dated, lower right

74. ***Mazzo di fiori sul tavolo rosa e grigio***, 1959
Bouquet with Pink and Gray Table

Mixed media
62.9 x 48.3 cm.; 24 3/4 x 19 inches
Signed and dated, lower right

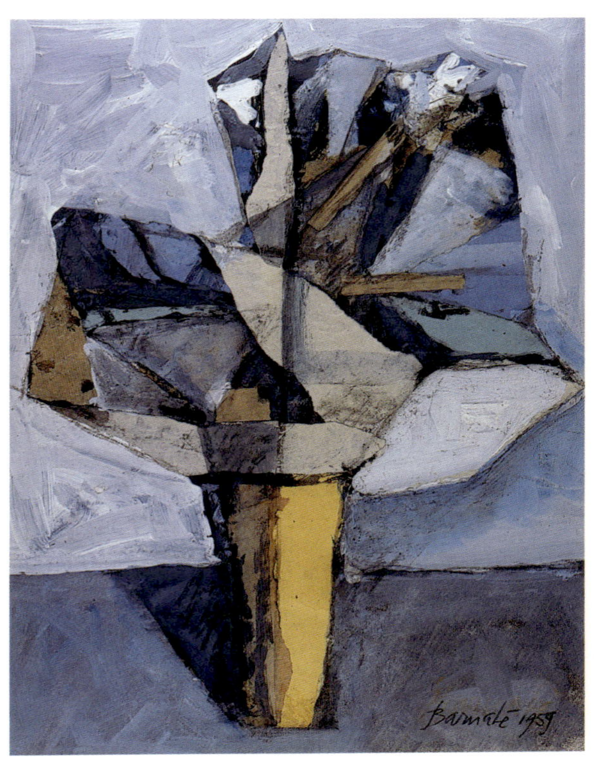

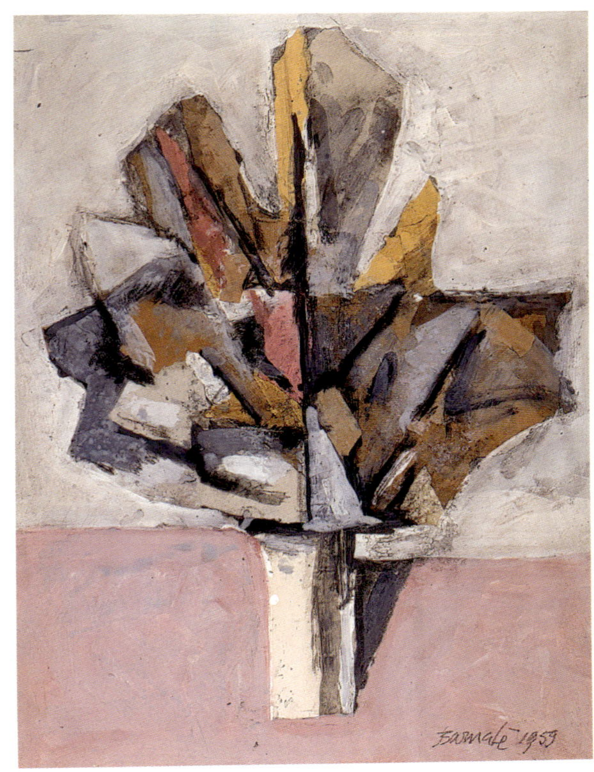

75. ***Cardinale su fondo rosso corallo***, about 1960
   Cardinal with Red Coral Background

   Oil on canvas
   130 x 97 cm.; 51 1/4 x 38 1/4 inches
   Signed, lower right

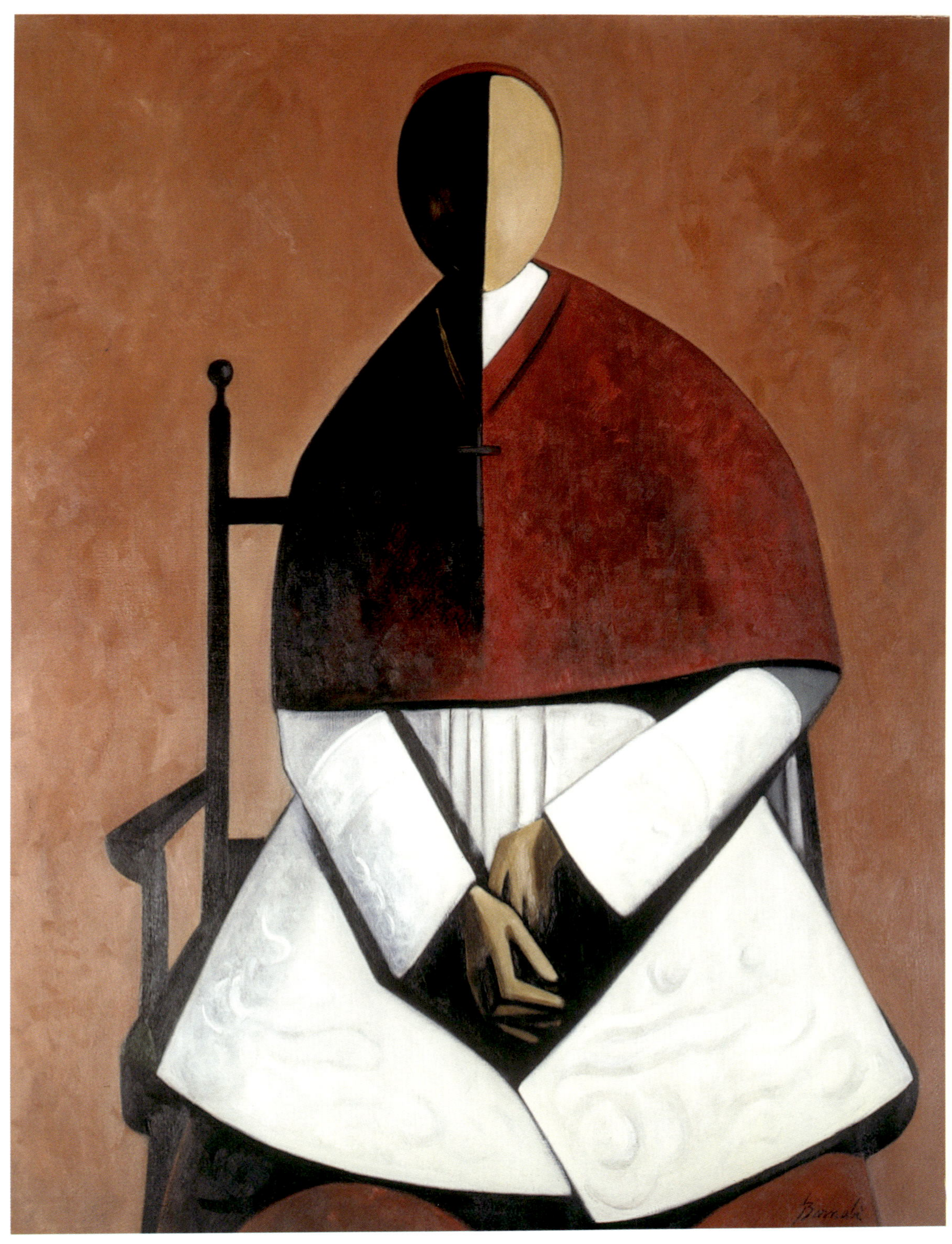

76. ***Natura morta con bilancia blu***, about 1960
Still Life with a Blue Scale

Oil on canvas
68.5 x 81 cm.; 27 x 32 inches
Signed, lower right

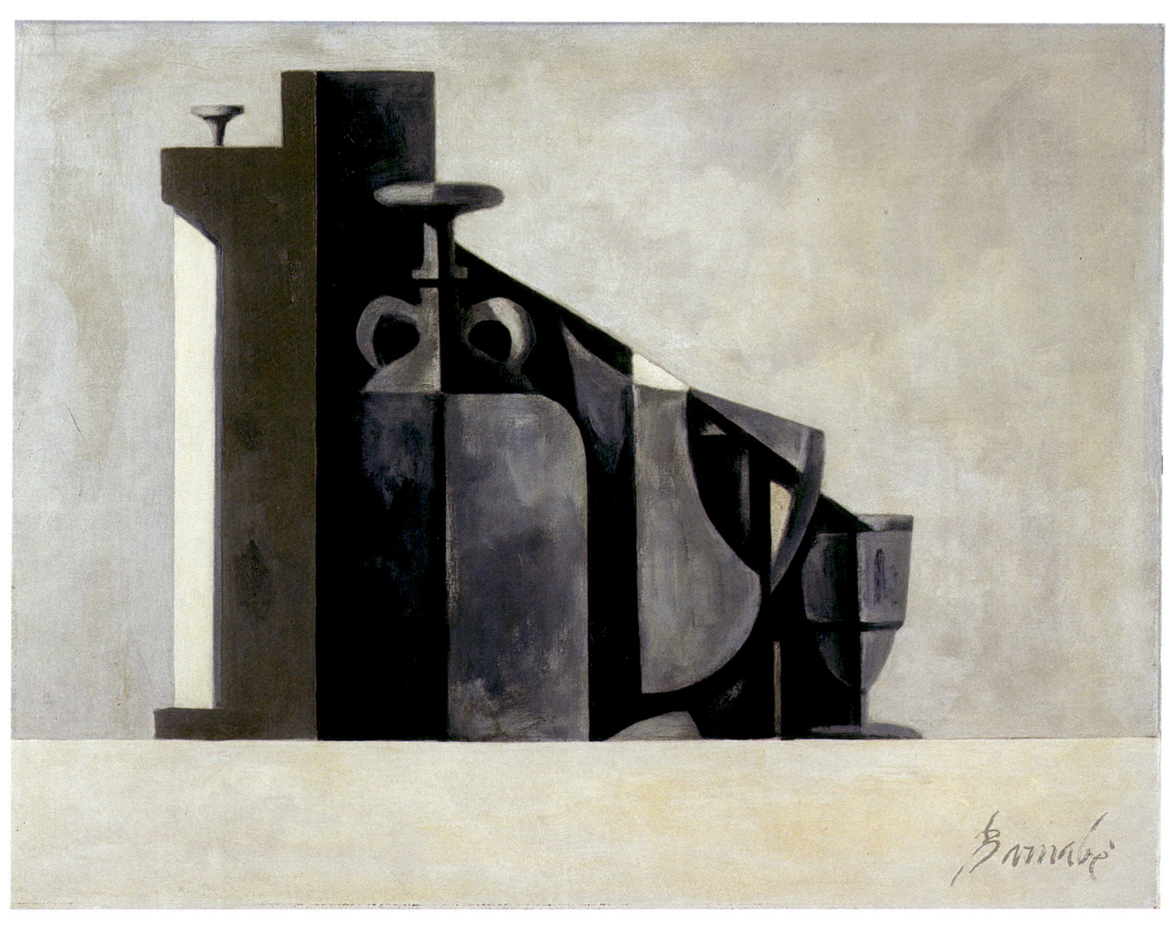

77. ***Pierrot con flauto***, about 1960
Pierrot with Flute

Oil on canvas
146 x 97.2 cm.; 57 1/2 x 38 1/4 inches
Signed, lower right

Collection:
Dan Fischel and Sylvia Neil

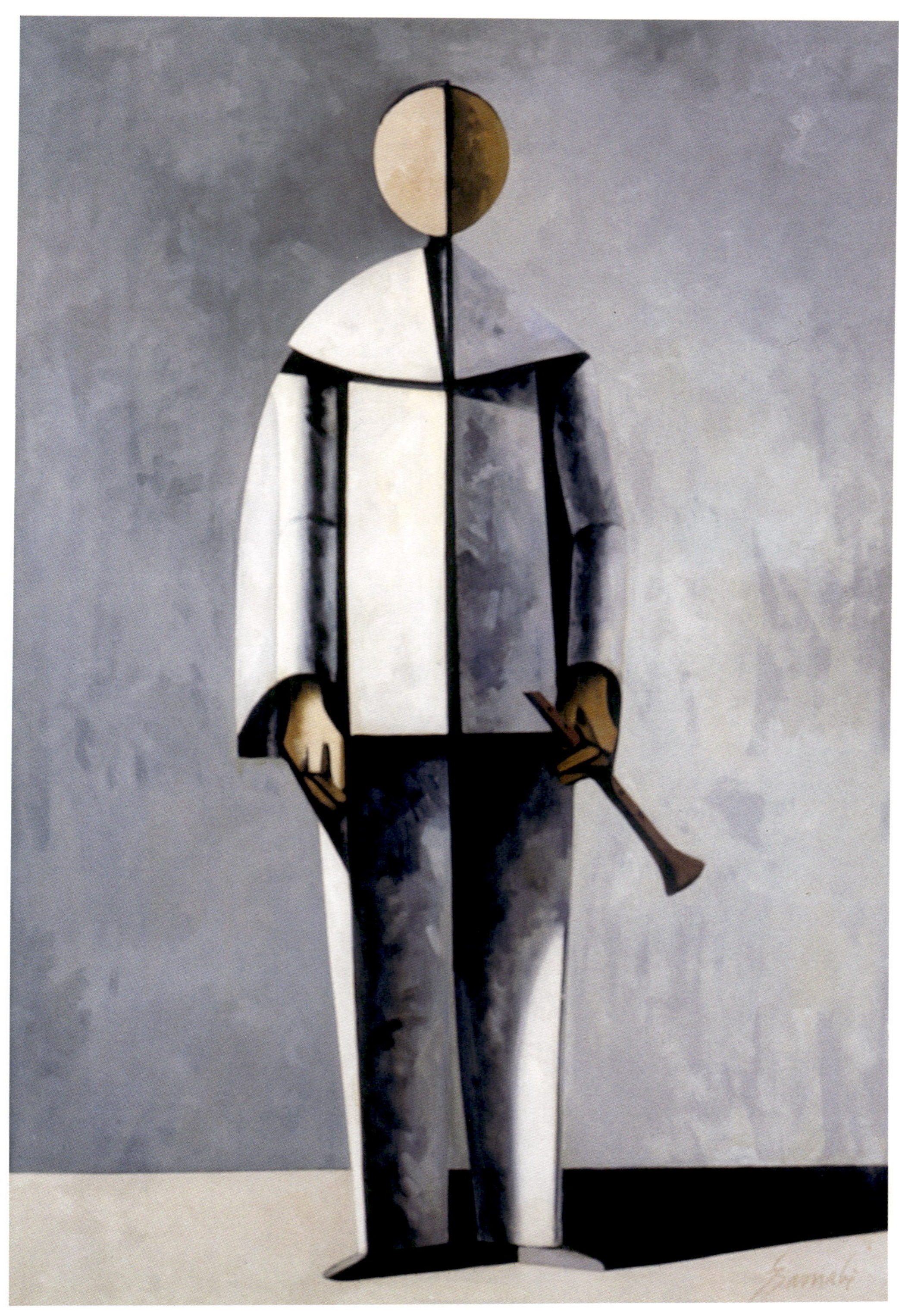

78. ***Mazzo di fiori ellittico,*** about 1960
Elliptical Bouquet

Charcoal
65.4 x 50.2 cm.; 25 3/4 x 19 1/2 inches
Signed, lower center

79. ***Mazzo di fiori,*** 1960
Bouquet

Charcoal
65.4 x 50.2 cm.; 25 3/4 x 19 3/4 inches
Signed and dated, lower center

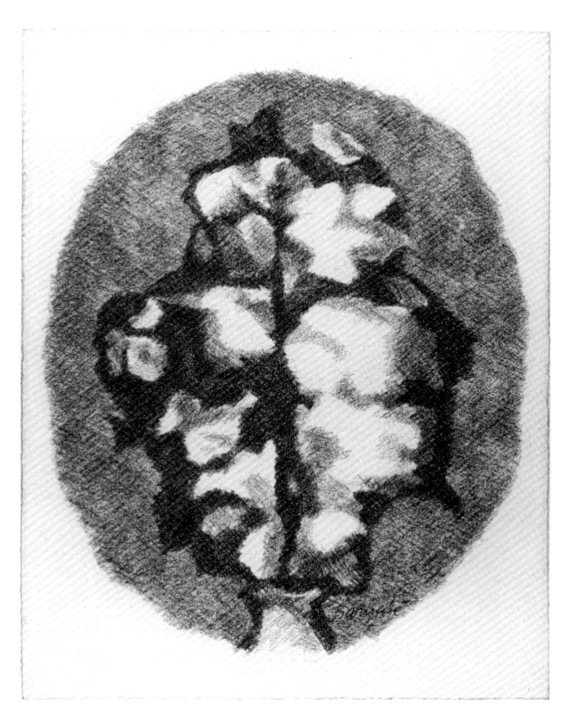

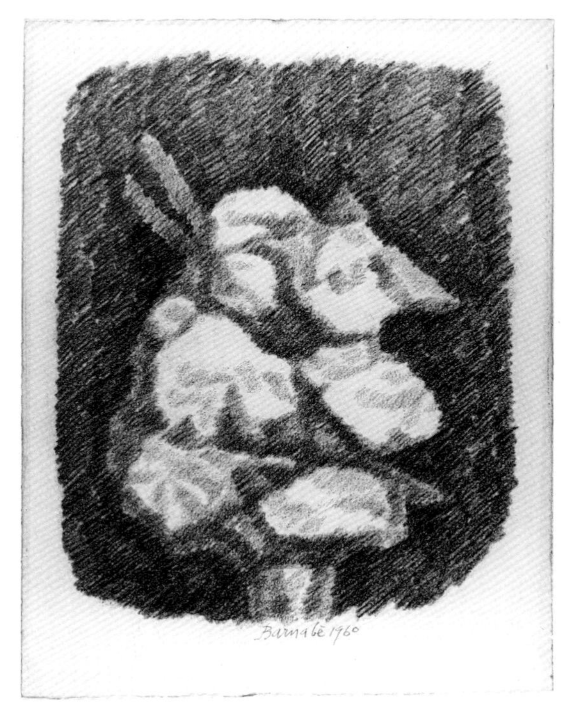

80. *Cardinale con rosario*, about 1961
    Cardinal with Rosary

    Oil on canvas
    100 x 81 cm.; 39 3/8 x 31 7/8 inches
    Signed, lower right

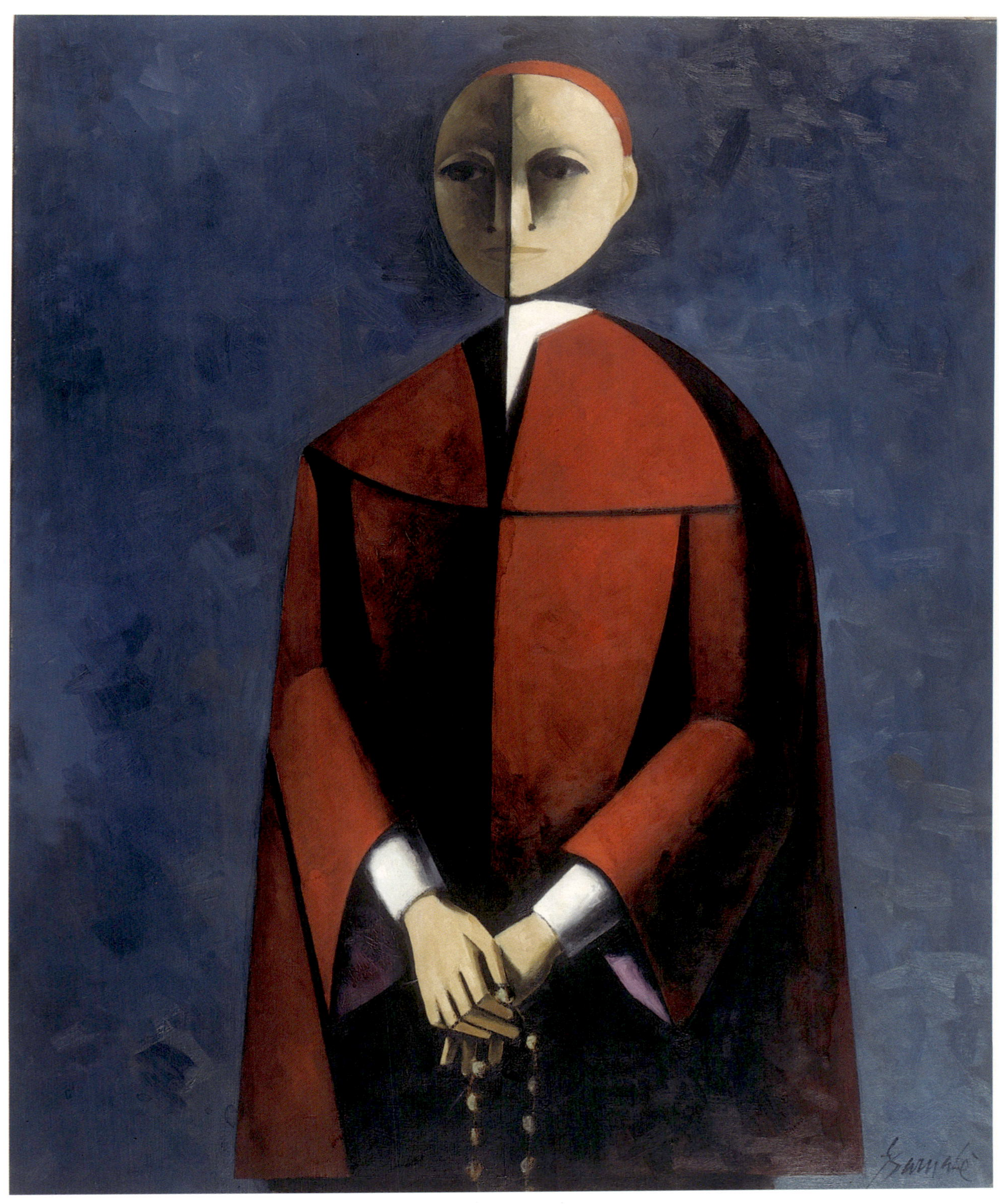

81. ***Piccolo mazzo di fiori***, about 1960
Little Bouquet

Charcoal
50.2 x 34.9 cm.; 19 3/4 x 13 3/4 inches
Signed, lower left

82. ***Mazzo di fiori con ombra,*** 1960
Shadowed Bouquet

Charcoal
65.4 x 50.2 cm.; 25 3/4 x 19 3/4 inches
Signed and dated, lower center

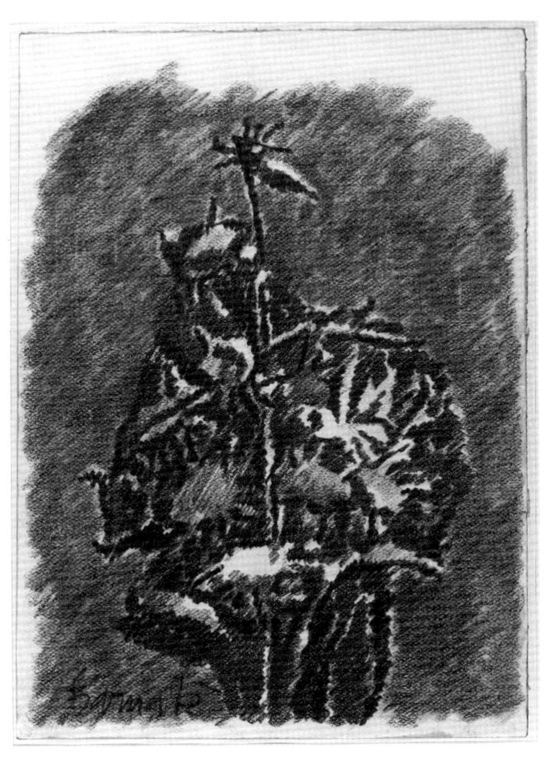

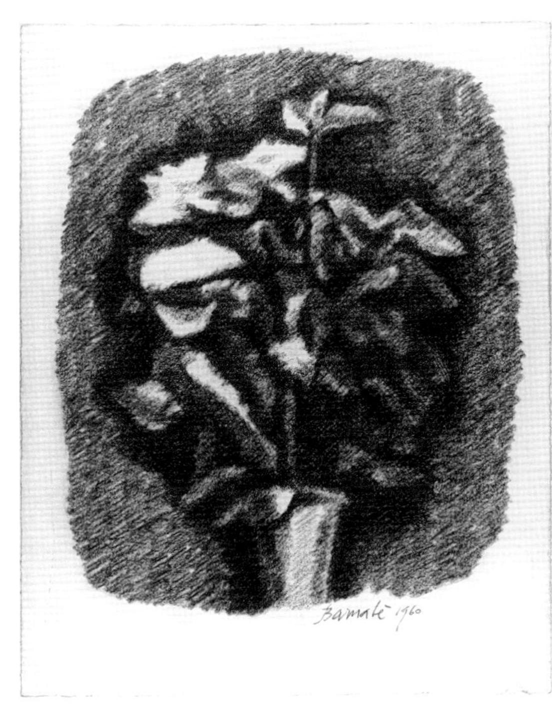

83. ***Ragazzo con anguria,*** 1961
Boy with Watermelon

Oil on canvas
130.2 x 97.2 cm.; 51 1/4 x 38 1/4 inches
Signed and dated, lower right

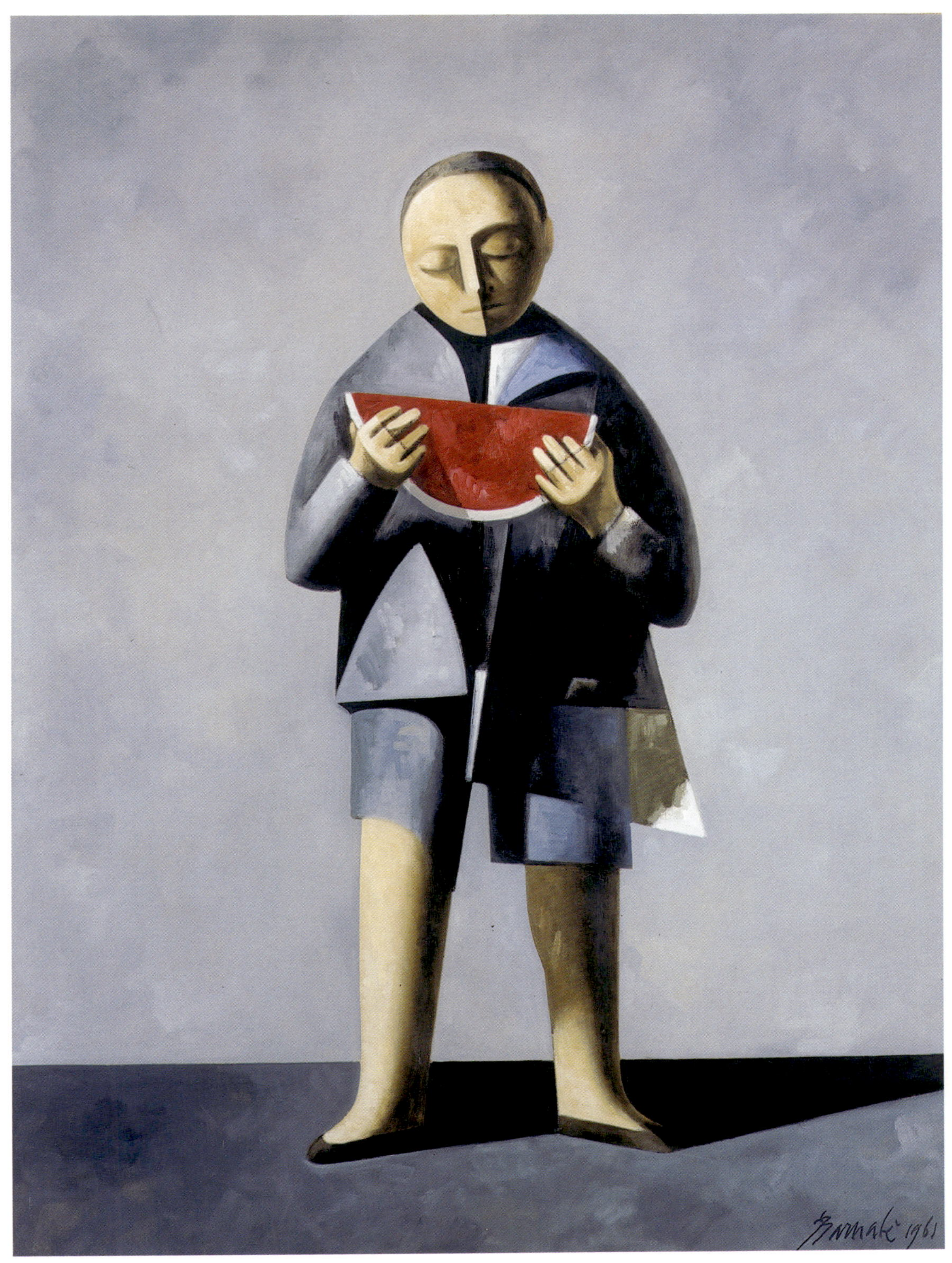

Barnato 1961

84. ***Chierighetto dell'Avvento,*** 1961
Advent Altar Boy

Oil on canvas
130.2 x 97.2 cm.; 51 1/4 x 38 1/4 inches
Signed and dated, lower right

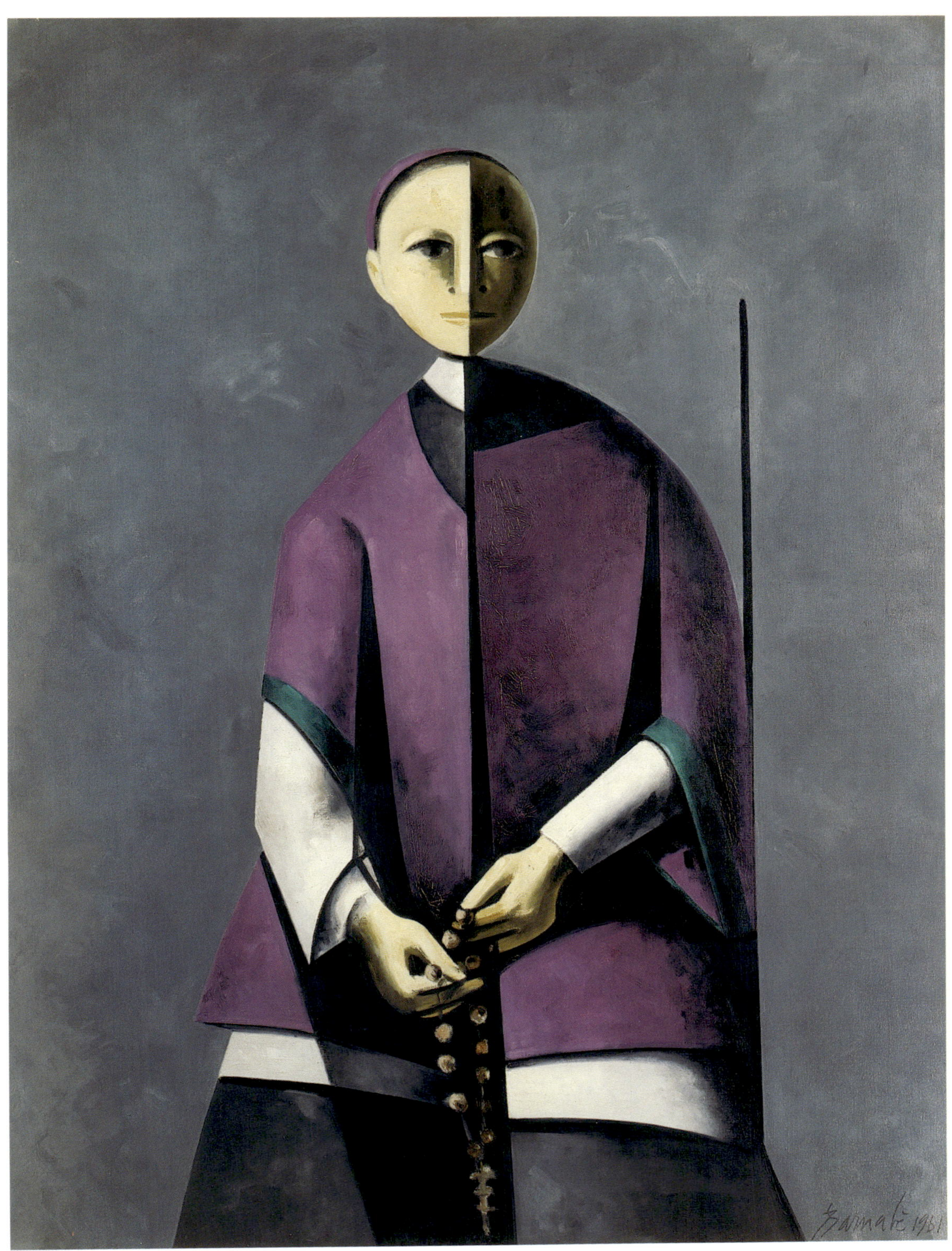

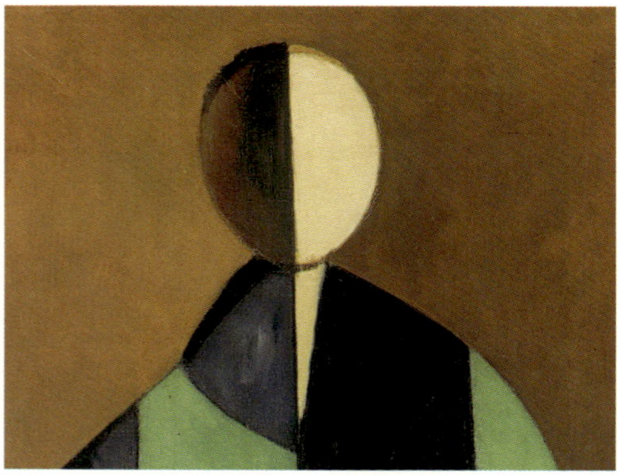

No. 47 (detail)